STILLMEADOW
CALENDAR

STILLMEADOW CALENDAR

A COUNTRYWOMAN'S JOURNAL

by Gladys Taber

with drawings by Sidonie Coryn

J. B. LIPPINCOTT COMPANY
PHILADELPHIA AND NEW YORK

Library of Congress Catalog Card Number: 67-11312

For Jill

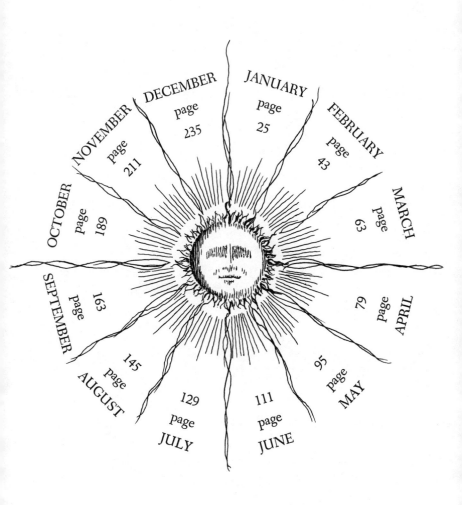

STILLMEADOW
CALENDAR

Foreword

THE COUNTRY ROAD winds along Jeremy Swamp Road to a crossroad with eight mailboxes in jagged array on posts. In winter the drifts rise high, so getting to the mailbox is a hazard, and in summer the Stillmeadow box is full of wasps. I suppose, if I were a wasp, I too would appreciate a weatherproof metal box, big and at good flying height. If you turn right at the mailboxes, you skirt the end of the swamp and come to a small white pre-Colonial farmhouse surrounded by giant sugar maples so high that the tops seem to interfere with the moon's course.

The house has two stories but looks like a one-story building due to the steep slant of the roof. In the time when this house was built, taxes were higher on two-story dwellings, so the settlers sensibly built to give the effect of only one story. Therefore, there are no second-story windows on the front, and the eaves are directly above the windows in the parlor and my room. The upstairs windows were let inconspicuously into the sides of the house.

Stillmeadow dates back to 1690; consequently it was built around a central chimney, which is fourteen feet square in the cellar. The foundation is dry-laid stone, and the supporting beams are hand-hewn chestnut. ("I'd as soon saw through cement," said a repairman one day.) The floor boards are wide, mostly black oak, and set with hand-cut nails with square heads. Batten doors swing on wrought-iron hinges throughout the house. The windows are twelve over eight (panes), and a few still have the bubbly glass. A little of the old plaster remains, rough in texture and rather bumpy. ("Won't take but a day or so to knock that down and put in nice smooth plaster, Mrs. Taber.")

The clapboards are hand-cut and cast wavering lines of shadow when the light is right. ("No, Mr. Barker, you cannot replace the cracked one. Patch it up.")

The roof, alas, puts the signature of this century on the house, but it can't be helped. It looks as much like the old mossy wooden one as could be managed. You hardly notice it anyway, for the maples overhang it and the lilacs reach up to it. The old well house was reroofed fifteen years ago, and the wisteria generously twines along the edges.

The land falls away on either side, to the swamp at right and to the pond at left. The thickets at the rear of the swamp give way to the woods, which climb a fairly steep hill. Except for two old apple orchards, the forty acres have only one open space, a small arable level piece suitable for crops and hay.

What kind of man built this house? We can only guess.

He was a careful man, for the hand-hewn beams in the family room are gently shaped and the hand-cut nails are remarkably alike. He was a wise man, for he set the house on a slight rise and built the chimney high enough to prevent downdrafts. He had a family. There are three bedrooms upstairs and the borning room downstairs, the parlor and a second room the same size, and the kitchen with the crane for cooking and the Dutch oven.

The borning room opens from the kitchen; presumably some heat seeped in for the baby and mother. It is the coldest room in the house, oil burner notwithstanding. The stairway is nothing, really, but a ladder with back to the treads and walls closing in tight on both sides. At the foot of it is the coffin door giving onto the back stoop. The early builders, knowing a coffin could never be turned at the bottom of the stairs, sensibly cut an extra door in the wall at the bottom.

Through this door went the coffin of one of the church elders around eighty or eighty-five years ago and was carried by men on foot all the way to the church, several miles away. I think of this when I drive to the church in four or five minutes.

In the 1700's another householder added a piece to the house with a milk room, a summer kitchen or workroom, and a shed which housed the facilities. When, down the years, plumbing came in, this became a woodshed.

Two upstairs closets or storage places eventually were made into bathrooms, and the milk room adapted itself to a new era with a refrigerator and a sink with running water. A black iron cookstove in the summer kitchen provided the housewife with another means of cooking than the fireplace, and it had a reservoir to heat water besides.

The people who owned Stillmeadow immediately preceding us were, as we were told, such nice people. It was too bad Mr. A was so nervous and shot his wife and then killed himself. It was especially too bad, as they had a house guest who had come from New York to rest from a nervous state of her own. Nothing indicates what happened to her. However, a good deal of debris was in the house, along with a good many unpaid bills and telegrams and letters, all of which I shamelessly read. It was a stormy and passionate love. Mr. A was in the service and his beautiful beloved was married to another man and lived, rather prosaically, in New Jersey. Mr. A called her Laurie, which was not her name, but much more romantic than her own. My favorite telegram said:

LAURIE, I AM GOING TO SEND YOU A TIGER. WATCH
FOR A LARGE CRATE.

After the war, the lovers were reunited (no mention of the husband). Mr. A suffered from shell shock, and they moved to the tranquil countryside for his health. They raised, as an avocation, fancy pheasants. Charles (that is not his name either) had a habit of appearing in doorways with a pheasant whose neck he had just wrung. Callers found this disturbing. One neighbor stopping by on business found Charles pulling a revolver from his hip pocket and threatening his wife, whereupon she snatched it from him and ran to the yard, firing it in the air as long as the bullets lasted. Then she laughed and threw it in the bushes.

It was all very sad, and they were such nice people. But the murder and suicide left the house empty while the tangled affairs of the estate were settled, and in the end it came on the market. Then it stood quietly waiting for life to begin again, for an ancient house has seen many sorrows as well as joys and is intimate with laughter and tears in equal measure. It has survived blizzards and hurricanes and fires in the attic and so many wars—who can now count them? The British burned Danbury but never got twenty miles further north. Rochambeau and the French troops camped seven miles away in Newtown but never drank from the well of a farmhouse tucked away in the low hills.

Stillmeadow's calendar began again on a February day during a paralyzing blizzard. The prospective owners came across the fields up to the waist in drifts while the realtor began digging out the car a quarter of a mile back. I've told this before, but every now and then one of the children says, "Tell how we got Stillmeadow!" And presently it will be time to tell the grandchildren.

The passion for a place in the country came simultaneously to Jill, my lifelong friend, and to me. We lived in New York City in apartments on the upper West Side. Don and Dorothy, Jill's son and daughter, were thin, leggy children, and my daughter Connie was thin, leggy, and pale. They didn't remotely resemble the rugged, vigorous children we had been at their age. We had grown up in Midwestern towns where every house had a huge yard and you could just walk to the edge of town and be in the woods or rolling rich fields. We were used to rivers nearby and lakes and camping.

Jill was working full time as a psychiatric social worker for the city, and I was studying and teaching at Columbia part time. The idea of a place in the country came one hot, dusty day as we sat on a bench in the park while the children just stood around like Joseph in the Cherry Tree Carol. It seemed suddenly practical to buy a cheap piece of land, put up a tent or a shack, and have week ends of fresh air and clean grass.

We found out very soon that no realtor within a reasonable distance of the city would bother with us. The real estate business is not a charitable institution. We went farther afield and inspected decayed Victorian mansions, remodeled barns with no plumbing. We learned that maple shade and a running brook meant just that and that when an ad said NEEDS SOME WORK, it did indeed.

During the two years of the great hunt, we had acquired a cocker spaniel (for me) and two for Jill. And a Siamese cat just happened to choose me. So we were en route to a dog show with the promising puppy when we stopped off to investigate one of the endless ads in the papers.

The realtor said he didn't have a key and doubted we could get through the road anyway, but we insisted. Our stubbornness paid off for once, because the next week end another buyer turned up and subsequently tried to buy the house from us for a small profit. That buyer had stayed home on account of the snowstorm.

We got in through the cellar door while the realtor kept on digging. To say the place was a mess is an understatement to end all understatements. The rats liked it, but the couple of birds that had flown down the chimney were very dead. Nevertheless the house said, "I've been waiting for you. It's time you came."

I imagine that restoring an old house, cherishing it, preserving it, and putting up with its quirks could be easy. The way to do it would be to sell a few thousand shares of IBM or AT&T and take a cruise around the world. While you climbed the pyramids, Mr. Clark would be climbing your roof, and while you visited Stratford on Avon, workmen would sardine themselves into every cranny of your house in the country. Designers and decorators would operate by remote control, and when you came back you would simply unpack. I have actually been in a few such houses and they are beautiful. The one thing they lack is memories of every hard-won struggle.

For instance, as I look at one spot in the softly waxed family-room floor, I can remember the cigarette tin that was tacked over the hole in it. When I look at the pale green and cranberry medallions of the Whistler wallpaper in the front parlor, I remember when we tore down the purple-and-pink-flowered paper and redid the room ourselves. Our first effort was a failure. We put on "The Landing of the Pilgrims," and in the narrow room the Pilgrims seemed to be landing on everyone's shoulders. That was an active room until we learned more about paper. As I take some crystal ice cubes from the purring refrigerator, I remember when the antique one we inherited just gave up and neon gas or whatever it was poured out all over the floor. We flung children, puppies, and cats out the kitchen door, and Jill slid in the front door to telephone for help.

We were disastrously short of money, but I am glad we were. We would never have learned to paper and paint, refinish furniture, raise vegetables and can them, make jelly enough to last for a year of jelly sandwiches.

Jill, far more able than I, became a good carpenter and furniture builder. The trestle dining table and long benches will last indefinitely. The walnut typing table she made for me supported a succession of typewriters (I wear them out). With the help of fifteen-year-old Phoebe, who worked for us one summer, she built a sturdy kennel for puppies. As we raised more and more cocker spaniels, she made extra kennel units in the barn.

We tried almost everything you can try in the country except that I refused to start having sheep to mow the lawn. I told her the cockers and the two Irish setters and the Siamese cat and the Manx would make sheep nervous. I gave in on the hens during the egg shortage period, and we had eighteen which we bought from a friend and lugged home in burlap bags. At once I grew attached to them and Jill eventually put the henhouse off limits for me because, as she said, we couldn't run a retirement home for hens, what with everything else, and they would have to end in the freezer. During this controversy, she mollified me by building the mushroom bed in the cellar so we could have the mushrooms we wanted.

This was not what the books call an unqualified success, for a mushroom bed begins with hot manure (you have to take its temperature), and my room was directly overhead, with plenty of wide cracks in those old floor boards. The mushrooms were lovely while they lasted—but that was not long.

The floors themselves were a problem. They rose and fell depending on the season. Jill would fill the cracks, crawling on hands and knees, and the floors would look fine until the weather changed and then the stuffing rose up and the boards sank. She tried glue, she tried ship's caulking, she tried a kind of pulverized wood, she tried pencil-thin pieces of board. She gave up after a winter spent filling the cracks with the newest and the best plastic compound. There is still some of that left, and the grandchildren love to creep along and poke out chunks and eat them. Adults keep a wary eye, but I wonder if my Anne doesn't have just a mite of crack filler in her anyway.

It would be good to be able to preserve the happy years, but they slip away. Jill died suddenly. Death sets its own schedule. The old house fell silent, no matter how many voices spoke sympathetic words. An army could have tramped through it, but without the sound of one steady footstep there might as well have been no sound whatever. My own footsteps seemed noiseless. A great many blank pages were turned on the Stillmeadow calendar while I slowly accustomed myself to walking another path.

Acceptance is an easier word to spell than to live by. It comes gradually—but come it must. I think happiness is living every day as completely as possible, spending it but not wasting it. And it isn't *what* happens as much as our attitude that matters.

Now at Stillmeadow the lilacs reach the roof. A friend once said, "Why not pick lilacs in the attic?" When we came, they were weak, stunted switches, for, I was told, Mr. A hated lilacs and was grubbing them out. Jill moved some of them, fed them lavishly, sprayed them for oyster scale. Now, they mark the passing time with new clusters of bloom every May. The flowering crab, once the size of a ruler, now spreads a rosy glow over the Quiet Garden. And ramblers cover the picket fence in June.

Growing is the natural law of life, and I like to think mankind as well as every other living thing is subject to it. I find the repeating pattern of nature a special reassurance that man may walk the valleys and climb the hills in the future as he has in the past. I have faith that tomorrow may yet be fair.

January

IT IS TIME to put up the new calendars, and as the old ones come down I wonder where the past year went. Some of it is now what Emily Dickinson would call "an amethyst remembrance." Perhaps some of it is better forgotten, but there is so much to remember and treasure. And as I open the calendar to January, I think that soon lilacs will be in bloom (just four pages away), and then the Spartan roses (two more pages); I remember that the children will be coming for visits, and the grandchildren will be celebrating their birthdays.

But right now, winter at Stillmeadow walks down the low hills and brims the meadows with her tides of snow. Some years, winter does more than arrive; she invades the valley. Then snow tops the picket fence; drifts are five feet deep. The whole landscape changes as the dune-shaped wind-rippled snow lies under a dark sky. There is a coldness, a purity, such as I seldom see, and landmarks vanish.

With waves of snow cresting around the old house, Jonquil and Teddy, the cockers, and Holly, the Irish setter, and

I feel like mariners. But we are fortunate, for we do not have to stand outside and mark a course. Instead, we sit by the open fire and have tea and cookies. I like to look out and see the pre-Revolutionary houses, anchored steadfastly. Summertime lights are not so lovely as winter lights on snow. If the road is deep with snow, I think how fortunate it is the house is snug. It is possible, if the furnace goes off, to keep the downstairs warm at Stillmeadow, but the upstairs is colder than outdoors. And the heat isn't what you would ever call even. Near the hearth it is tropical, but three feet away you begin to shiver. Always, when the weather is bitter, I wonder how the early settlers managed in drafty cabins heated only by fireplaces.

In my memory, 30 degrees below zero was the coldest we have had, but I am sure some old-timer can correct me. But there is this about our winter: the big drops do not last long, and then it seems quite balmy when the temperature is 38 degrees.

The new year often comes in accompanied by steeply falling temperatures and spitting snowstorms. In the city there is a lot of what Mama used to call "carrying-on." When the children were away at school or working in the city, Jill and I had a number of New Year's Eves by ourselves. We had a strong feeling of wanting to see the old year out beside our own fire, so we avoided the customary parties. We sometimes read aloud, we played our favorite records, and we talked about the year to come. I think of those New Year's Eves and am thankful we did not waste them while she was alive.

New Year's at Stillmeadow is a family occasion. Jill's daughter Dorothy and her husband Val and their two wonderful children come and fill the house with love and laughter. After dinner, the children toast marshmallows and pop corn over the open fire. The cockers like marshmallows and popcorn too, and Holly hangs around the kitchen waiting for more turkey. After the children climb the ladder stairs and go to bed, the three of us settle down for a warm and comfortable talk. Jill used to say, "There is one thing about us, we are a verbal family." So we are!

Midnight comes all too soon, and we bring in a tray with freshly baked sourdough bread with cheese and salami and thin slices of ham and pickles. When the chimes ring out (over television to be sure), we hold hands and say our private prayers for the year to come. I couldn't wish for a better way to begin than this.

I abhor leave-takings. When the holiday season ends and the children leave, when the last hunt for missing toys is over and the last mittens are found, when the car vanishes down the road, there is a dreadful stillness in the house. The change from gay chaos to ordered living is not easily made.

My antidote for that desolate feeling is to begin cleaning the house. Even if the children leave at night, with the small fry already in bunny pajamas and ready for bed, I get busy at once, attacking the counters and removing layers of peanut butter and jelly. I mop the melted snow from the back kitchen floor and toss what seem to be a million towels and forgotten shirts and socks in the washing machine. I pick up educational toys and apple cores and I wax the trestle table, which is thickly covered with debris. A couple of hours of hard work bring me a sense of accomplishment and a feeling that life is still going on. What I can never do in the first loneliness is concentrate on a book or get back to the typewriter. I remember how my mother used to scrub the cellar steps in times of trouble, and I suppose I am like her.

I begin the new year with plenty of wood cut and stacked by my neighbor Joe Vanek. Joe is a true lover of the land, and he never cuts a straight living tree. Most of my forty acres and much of his farmland are wooded, and there are always trees which nature herself is discarding according to her laws. Most farmers have woodlots and cut with care, thinning when necessary but always saving the woods. We are natural conservationists if we depend on the land; we do not lay it waste.

The firewood burns brightly these days. January in New England requires stamina. Going anywhere is a hazard, and Arzie Bennett spends most of his time getting out the truck and rescuing stalled cars. Sometimes a neighbor has a dinner party for ten, and only three manage to get there. But then there are still, clear nights when the roads are all plowed (we plow according to what roads are hard-surfaced and what are dirt roads). My road is usually the last since it doesn't go anywhere but up the hill. When I hear the swish of snow and the beat of the engine on the plow, I feel I am introduced to the world again. The urge to go to the village, to Woodbury, to Newtown is strong.

To be out, just doing ordinary errands, is a joy after being housebound! However, I have learned to leave the dogs at home when the roads are bad. In case I get stuck, I cannot trudge for help with a bevy. Holly takes it hardest. She has her signature all over the top of the cherry table by the front window. Teddy sits on the window sill. Jonquil just paces. But all of them greet me warmly at the door with swirling ears and beating tails and with presents which range from the best sofa pillow to my slippers and an ash tray.

But we New Englanders take weather as it comes. Recently a friend remarked that New Englanders must be mad to live in such a climate. "Freeze in January, boil in July," she said. I protested that June and October are very reliable, and that every month has its own beauty. When it is bitter cold, I enjoy the song of the open fire on the old hearth; the song of the winter birds at the feeders; the humming of the tea kettle; the stamping of a neighbor's boots on my doorstep. And nothing can compare with the sunset over a world of white.

I think the climate of home—wherever it may be—is always what we most like. There are more benign climates than mine, but I am satisfied with New England, which can sometimes be one of the most difficult places of all, practically speaking. Right now, for instance, I deplore not being able to get fresh lettuce, which is so good with the dressing my friend Kay Barker makes. The recipe calls for 1 pint of mayonnaise or salad dressing, ½ pound of bleu cheese, ½ pint of light cream, ¼ cup of milk, and ⅛ cup of French dressing. If you have a blender, the dressing goes in and out faster than you can count. If not, it beats well with an ordinary beater. This is a dressing I could eat with a spoon.

Around four in the afternoon the day's activity is over, and the cockers are ready for a doze by the fire. Night comes so early that supper is by lamplight. I really prefer the long summer days, for I love light with a passion. I should qualify this, for I enjoy night when it is *supposed* to be night—midnight, for instance. But I want my days brimming with light. I would have made a sorry cave dweller and no doubt would have met an early end sneaking out of the cave to look at the open sky.

Sometimes days are so dark I have the lights on; but then the sky opens her door as the sun goes down and an apricot fire burns over the hills. But winter sunsets do not linger, and soon the wolf moon rises.

I build up the fire and start supper. If it is very cold, I hook up the electric light on an extension cord and lay it near the pipes in the back kitchen and turn a small electric heater on the sink plumbing. When I look out the back window, I see the icicles hanging from the old well. The wisteria is a pattern of ice-lace. Gibran says, "If winter should say, 'Spring is in my heart,' who would believe winter?"

Later, a walk in the moonlight is a fine thing, but few walk far because the January air has a killing blade on a clear night. The fire on the hearth is especially welcome, and I love to gather friends or the family around it, and pop corn and eat polished apples, and listen to Bernstein's recording of Tchaikovsky's "1812 Overture," which Ted, my musician friend, says is corny—but oh so beautiful. I even love the cannons booming toward the end!

When I was on Cape Cod, I went one day to call on a quail. As I was about to leave the house, the phone rang and someone asked if I was going to be in.

"I'm very sorry," I said innocently. "You see, I'm just off to visit a quail."

There was a startled silence.

"Her name is Robert," I explained. I thought that would clear things up.

Robert presided over the household of Dr. and Mrs. Kienzle at Orleans. A few years ago, after a bad storm, they found two eggs in an abandoned nest. One was broken, but they took the other one into the house, washed it with water, and, as Mrs. Kienzle adds apologetically, sprayed it with insecticide. They left it on the kitchen counter and went to the living room; when they came back, Mrs. Kienzle exclaimed, "Look, it's moving!"

And so it was. In a day or two they watched the eggshell being neatly opened in a circle. Out came Robert, about the size of a bumblebee. The first time I saw her, she was ten weeks old and very sociable. She followed along like a dog, rode happily on any shoulder, or cuddled in cupped hands. All the time she talked softly—in a gentle conversational coo. She played curious little games, almost dancing around a shoe. Her first bed was a snug carton with a boudoir light placed at one end to keep out the chill. An old lamb's-wool duster hung down the other end, and she snuggled inside the lamb's-wool part. A door sign read: BOBBY WHITE.

Quail are beautiful birds, and a quail in the hand is a miracle of muted colors—more than I could count. The trusting, candid eyes are not black but a shining brown. The two white bars on the head are like chalk lines. Most wild creatures respond to any human kindness. I wish we had more of it. . . .

One reason for the beauty of New England is the architecture, for the houses and churches were built to fit the land and the climate. The small-paned windows kept out the bitter cold, as did the low-hung doors; the steep pitch of roofs sheds heavy snow, and low eaves shed the melt easily. The houses lower as staunch as the sailing ships that went out from Gloucester, New Bedford, Provincetown. There was no gingerbread decoration. But the fanlights that were over front doors had grace, and the shutters, which could be locked when needed, gave design to the plain houses. In the Victorian period some of the beautiful dwellings were "done over" with unfortunate results, and now owners tend to remove the ugly porches and fretwork, bringing the houses back to simple loveliness.

Time certainly brings about changes. I have been thinking about a statement I read that if we had all the electric appliances we could use in the home, there would be 166 of them. Well, this includes *everything*. I can't help sneaking a look around to see how many I have, and as I go from my room to the back kitchen I note that one counter has a coffeemaker, toaster, electric skillet (which I dearly love), and blender—plus the refrigerator plug and a plug for the steam iron. But, I tell myself, Stillmeadow was home down through the years for many people who had no appliances at all. And I still like to cook over the open fire, hanging my iron Dutch oven from the same crane that was used by the first lady of the house almost three hundred years ago. It seems like a bond between her and me. And I enjoy lighting a very old kerosene lamp that was given to me long ago. The base is pale-green pressed glass, and the chimney is fluted. It gives a soft, delicate glow.

There is, I have found, at least one good or lovely thing in every single day. Everyone has sorrow, endures difficult times, but loveliness abides if we look for it. I almost forgot this the time I wrenched my knee and was flat for two weeks. I picked the worst time, too, for Erma Vanek, my mainstay, was down with a virus. Joe, her husband, had to take on all of their chores, besides his regular job. The weather was terrible. It does seem as if things pile up sometimes. I helped matters by getting bursitis in both shoulders from trying to make my way to the kitchen (despite that wrenched knee), clinging to furniture tops for support. After that bout, I found I could not even turn over in bed.

Of course, this wasn't a major disaster, but when you live alone, walking assumes extra importance, and I felt very low after my unsuccessful attempt. And then, just at the worst moment, in walked my neighbor, Wilma Phillips, bringing my mail. She let the dogs out, let them in, fixed me a tray, and lugged my books over near my bed so that I could reach them. And at six that night my bedroom door opened: there was Steve Nies—from up the hill—with a hot dinner wrapped in foil. His mother had dished mine up with theirs, and the sugar-sweet ham, fluffy potatoes, and fresh peas were flanked by an artistic salad. Dessert was in a foil cup. I have seldom had a happier time. Long after I forgot the misery of the pain, I felt the warm glow of friendship. By the time I could hobble, I felt like a queen.

George, at the market, offered to bring me, personally, any groceries I needed. Dick Gracy, from the Main Road, brought my newspaper right into the kitchen and hauled supplies. Joe carried wood, opened stuck windows, and went to the woods to pick me the loveliest bouquet of spring flowers I have ever seen. So, when I finally landed in the hospital, I had plenty of courage for that.

This being my first time out of circulation, except for brief bouts with grippe, I learned something important. It isn't the occasional grand gesture that matters so much. My neighbors were never too busy *every day* to pop in and look after me. The first minute Erma could get out of bed and weave over, bringing my favorite chicken soup as only she makes it, I was able to assure her I was fine, even if I could only take four steps.

I have several very dear friends who tell me they expect nothing but trouble. I do not go along with this. I do not believe in living trouble before it happens. I prefer to remember the loving-kindness of friends and expect this never to fail. I believe life is rich and rewarding, provided we accept it.

When the children were here on a visit a while ago, I gave a party during the course of which two friends said that my little granddaughter Anne, a lively curly-haired, blue-eyed pixie of a person, looks exactly like me. This really gave me what they used to call a turn. On the one hand, I felt they might better have thought she resembled Miss America; but on the other hand, a wave of pure happiness washed over me. And since I can never conceal anything, one guest said, "Just look at the way she looks! Simply glowing!"

And I think my feeling was that truly this wonderful, enchanting morsel was possibly in some small way my own. It was a special gift. I wondered weakly whether it would be all right to hunt up a baby picture of me, the one in the blue bonnet! But Anne bustled in with a green bath towel, which she said was a "cosy nest," and she worked away spreading it flat, which involved endless trips around and around pulling and tugging. Then she plopped down on it flat, spread out to the edges. "Ho-kay," she remarked. And whom she resembled was a very academic question!

In January, I am housebound part of the time and there are two ways to look at it. One, it is lonely; but two, it means long hours of work on a book because I have no excuse not to be working! When Jill was alive, it was no problem, for I could always hear her hammering away and sanding something in the back kitchen or dropping things as she reorganized the kitchen cupboards. Now I tend to look out of my window frequently after three in the afternoon so I can catch the lurid light of the school bus stopping up the hill.

Then I see my young friend Tommy plunging down the road. He is thin and leggy, with blazing hair and the blue eyes that go with it. If often the weather is very bad, he calls his mother to say he is back. They live, fortunately, just around the corner. Fortified with hot cocoa and cookies, Tommy fares forth to fill the bird feeders, run with the dogs, bring in wood, shovel the new fall of snow. It is my opinion every household needs a boy on hand for many reasons. But especially for companionship.

When I go out for a walk with the cockers and Holly, I sometimes look to see how many branches came down in the last ice storm. Winter does her own pruning. And I think that, as the new year begins, I might well do some pruning in my own life, keeping the essentials, the real values, and letting go the part that is no longer contributing to the growing time of my spirit.

The giant sugar maples are so high that I get dizzy if I look up and try to see the tops. Squirrels scamper from branch to branch, while woodpeckers hammer away. As I gaze at the trees, I think they are lovelier than when tented with green. In the blue twilight they are empty, but on still days they are filled with winter birds. On sunny mornings, when I go out to the feeders, they come and perch on nearby branches to watch breakfast being served. The chickadees talk the most, and I wonder how so much sound can come from such minute beings. The blue jays are loudest, with a peculiarly harsh voice, and when they flash in, the gentle snowbirds vanish. They are not immoral, for there is no such thing in nature, but they dominate the winter world. Their sapphire blue is the most colorful hue my feathered residents display.

What the new year will bring, we cannot know. I think of the year that has been folded away in time. There has been much good in it, although some sorrow. But there are always, in any year, many lovely memories, and I shall cherish them. Life is not, for most of us, a pageant of splendor but is made up of many small things, rather like an old-fashioned piecework quilt. No two people have the same, but we all have our own, whether it be listening to Beethoven's Fifth with a beloved friend or seeing a neighbor at the back door with a basket of white dahlias. Or after a long, hard day having the family say, "That was a good supper."

As the clock moves irrevocably from yesterday to today, I go out on the terrace and fill my heart with the intensity of the winter moonlight. This is the time when the heart is at peace and the spirit rests. I think of the words, "Be still, and know that I am God." Far off a branch falls in the old orchard, and sometimes a plane goes overhead bound for a far destination. I wish the pilot well, in that cold sky, and hope the passengers come safely home. Silently I say, "Happy New Year to all of us, all over this turning earth. And may we make it a year of loving-kindness and gentle hearts."

Sidonie Coryn

February

BUTTERMILK PANCAKES with first-run maple syrup belong to February breakfasts, and guests come and go, depending on the snow. There is this to be said about February at Stillmeadow: the signs of spring are here. The white horses of winter still pound down the valley, but the end of the course is in sight. For example, I wade through melting snow to the pond and find the tips of skunk cabbage poking up where the brook runs in. I don't know why, but they remind me of medieval hooded monks. Later, they look absurdly tropical with their rank green growth. Now I can imagine that if I lifted a hood I would see bright eyes looking at me. "See," they would say, "winter is never the end."

Names are curious. The skunk cabbage is elegant, but its name is not. I like names that bring out the best attribute of a plant. A New Jersey friend writes that they have always called lady's-slippers "whippoorwill's-shoes," and I find that charming. It's just *better* than lady's-slippers.

And now the sap runs. As I watch the slow flow of it down the trunks of the sugar maples, I think perhaps I should put in a spile and make just a little syrup. But I know better, because I still remember the disastrous results the year Jill decided to make syrup. All that sap going to waste, said she. When we later figured the cost of redoing the kitchen (the steam took off all the paint), cooking the sap day and night, and buying more pails and extra kettles, we found that a pint of our liquid gold cost more than an equal weight of pearls! We also were tired out, because you must keep sap boiling. You can never go to bed and forget it. You sit up. When people complain to me about the cost of pure maple syrup, I suggest they try making it once.

It is, however, a beautiful process. Along the valley roads, now, every great maple wears a shining tin pail like an ornament. In the moonlight farmers come out to empty the silvery fluid. Farmers, I think, move with a rhythm almost like that of an ancient ritual dance. To me the sight of a farmer swinging a scythe has more beauty than the gyrations of some modern dancers. For some modern dancing seems to involve twisting the body in all directions at once, just to prove it can be done. I suppose it expresses this contorted age, but I'd rather see patterns of movement that have beauty.

I have never seen a ground hog in February. Sometimes Joe brings me the news that we shall have six more weeks of winter or that spring is to be early. I am a firm believer in the truth underlying country legends, but I do not know why this one started. Who first saw a ground hog coming out and seeing his shadow and then counted the weeks just on a hunch? Hal Borland's theory is that ground hogs come out early if they get too hungry, not having been stuffed before hibernating. But there is a balance in nature, and perhaps spring is earlier when harvest time was poor.

Jonquil and Teddy, and Holly too, busy themselves in the yard all day, going through the snow like earnest bull-dozers. To me, the lovely light of February is a constant delight, and the dogs respond to it too. Holly races madly around the house, her Irish banner flying, and the cockers follow, never quite keeping up—but always trying nevertheless. Jonquil especially takes the light like a spring tonic and wags so hard and so long that I wonder her morsel of a tail can stand it!

When they come in, Holly sometimes gets stuck in the doorway: she is bringing in a branch as a treasure and it's too wide for the door. When she finally goes sideways with it, she leaves it on my bed. (When she's busy doing something else, I put it on the fire—a fine contribution to the economy of Stillmeadow!) The cockers come in looking like snowballs. They move toward the open fire and begin to steam a bit; then balls of ice plop to the floor fast. The smell is distinctly of wet fur! Occasionally, if they have been out chasing things too long, they have to curve themselves into chewing position and chop at the ice: for some reason they prefer to do this work themselves. I used to meet them at the back door with a bath towel, but they swept right past me and went to the fire. On the other hand, when they get briers in their fur after romping at the edge of the yard near the swamp, they press against me invitingly and suggest that it would be nice if I got out the scissors.

My father, who loved our family Irish, Timmie, so dearly, always referred to dogs as "large, unsanitary pets." This maintained his stature as a hard, firm man and meant he could secretly plant a kiss on Timmie's silken head when nobody was looking. Long after Timmie died at sixteen, I got another Irish setter and Father was horrified; he said I was unfaithful.

Dogs, I have found, tend to behave as their owners do. Most of the nervous, jumpy, snapping dogs I have known had a social environment that was about like that. A quiet, loving household means a sensible, well-mannered dog. A dog that seems super-intelligent has usually been talked to, played with, petted a lot (I hug mine), and generally treated like a loved person. A dog shut up in a pen and ignored will lack personality. I do not mean that heredity isn't also a factor, for when we raised cockers we were amazed to find Little Sister so exactly like Big Sister (Stillmeadow High Heritage). Especially Me, known as Teddy, resembles his mother and his father to an astounding degree. And Melody was as capricious and charming and flighty as Dark Star.

For the dogs, there are never any endings. There is always a new track in the snow to follow when the elusive rabbit has vanished. Something will turn up even when the six partridges have left the pine tree. I thought about this one night as I was stirring the split-pea soup for supper. I decided the secret of happy living is to keep a few beginnings on hand. The happy people I know are always beginning something—it doesn't much matter what it is. It may be making a rug or painting woodwork or planting new things or starting a new play group for children; there is no limit to what it can be, as long as it's a new project.

For instance, planning flower gardens. I love seed catalogues. I always cut out the gayest pictures of flowers I shall never be able to raise and pin them up in the kitchen to admire while I am getting meals. When we first came to Stillmeadow, both Jill and I were complete innocents. We ordered everything that looked lovely in the catalogues. It took us a number of years to learn the facts of gardening. Some things will grow for you; some will not. Climate is not something to ignore, nor is consistency of soil, nor location. Most of our shrubs were perambulatory as Jill moved them from shade to sun from rocky soil to loam, from sheltered to exposed spots.

"I am going to move the mock orange one more time," she would say, "and put the primroses on the south side of the border."

Now my main problem is to keep the house from being engulfed in a jungle. I plant nothing but spring bulbs, which don't keep reaching out and tangling with other things. For the rest, Erma comes down the road from her house about this time of year to tell me firmly that this spring things just must be *cut back*. She is a natural gardener, and Joe could set up as a nurseryman any minute. Between them, they have kept the house visible.

During February's brief thaw come gentle days when I gather sprays of pussy willow and dream of the green season. Others cut branches of quince and forsythia to bring indoors to bloom.

I have given up on the forsythia, because all mine do is leaf out. Jill planted our bushes long ago, and they grew

48

with the vigor of ragweed. When they put forth only one pale blossom, she consulted a garden authority. He advised moving them to a different location. She did. Those bushes are especially well traveled, having been all over the yard. In due time, another adviser inspected the single weak blossom each plant usually produced and advocated serious pruning. They were pruned. Nothing has ever stopped their fierce growth, but nothing has made them the golden shower they should be in spring. Across the road, untended bushes bear dazzling blooms.

The forsythia was Jill's only garden defeat, and she took it hard. Even the fact that she had a border of primroses that astonished the nurseryman didn't comfort her. It was her theory that the forsythia didn't like her.

I have been sorting books, this being a February job. I make a firm resolve annually to keep poetry in one part of the bookshelves, country books in another, classics on a low level for easy reaching, reference books very near my desk, fiction by itself. The way it ends is that I have two of my beloved Beverley Nichols books right in with Emily Dickinson and *Wuthering Heights*. As an organizer I am a washout. Should Keats's *Letters* be with Katherine Mansfield or along with Keats's poetry and *The Making of a Poet*? And where does James Thurber go? I do a lot of happy random reading while I am at this job; otherwise the results are just more confusion.

Sorting jobs are fun for Holly and the cockers. Just as I

have three piles laid on the bed, they all leap in the middle and do an egg-beater act. So then we go outdoors and fill the bird feeders. I decide the books are all right on any shelves at all.

The chickadees and juncoes and woodpeckers agree. This is a hard month for them, and I wish I could rig up an endless conveyor belt from the kitchen and keep pouring food on it. A friend told me that if I soaked raisins in warm water before putting them out, the birds would love them. Up to that time, I had given up on raisins. My birds are fussy and do not care for wild-bird mixtures. They eat the sunflower seeds in a mad rush and leave the rest. But they like chick-feed corn, so I buy it in twenty-five-pound lots. Mixed liberally with the sunflower seeds, nothing goes to waste: I have one friend who puts any leftovers out on a flat feeding station, from apple pie to pot roast. I think she found scalloped potatoes with onions the only menu nobody liked!

Valentine's Day, as I say annually, is almost my favorite holiday. I do not like funny cards for it, although for some occasions I find the offbeat cards a delight. Such as the one I received from my friend Helen, which said: NO, I DO NOT WISH YOU WERE HERE. On the inside it said, in small print: I WISHT I WAS THERE.

But for Valentine's Day the rosebuds and violets, the sentimental messages, are best. Of course, I am a highly consistent person, for my favorite remembrance last year was a load of wood from my friends! Moreover, they not only brought it in their station wagon; they stacked it! I found this, oddly enough, a romantic present, for it was a gift of warm fires on the open hearth.

And every four years, February strikes another romantic note—when Leap Year adds an extra day to the calendar. According to the Encyclopaedia Britannica the origin of the custom of allowing the so-called gentle sex to do the courting is a mystery. However, it goes back as far as 1288 when Scotland passed a law to the effect that "for ilke year known as lepe year, ilk mayden ladye of bothe highe and lowe estait shall hae the liberte to bespeke ye man she likes, albeit he refuses to taik hir to be his lawful wife, he shall be mulcted in ye sum ane pundis or less, as his estait may be." A few years later France adopted the same law, and in the fifteenth century Genoa and Florence followed suit.

What is especially interesting to me is that in this one respect all "maydens" were equal. The right to woo in Leap Year was given princess and peasant. I like to imagine a lady's maid and her mistress sallying forth to court the pageboy and the lord simultaneously. Well, after all, love knows no class distinctions!

During the last severe storm I decided to take a whole day of rest. I wasn't, I decided, going to do a single thing but rest and read. Kind of a house vacation. I began very well by staying in bed very late. Of course I got up at eight o'clock to let Holly out and at eight-thirty to let her back in, all fringed with snow and sleet. But after I toweled her dry, I went back to bed. Then I got up and fixed a good breakfast of French toast, baby sausages, cranberry juice, and coffee. So far, it seemed a fine program. Then I had to build the fire up, and this involved taking out the ashes, which meant cleaning the floor because a lot of them sifted all over it. Then I settled down to read *The Blue Lantern,* by Colette, reading as slowly as possible to savor every crystalline word (but I cannot, cannot read slowly). In about an hour I had more coffee and noted that the coffeepot needed cleaning. This is a chore because it is an automatic coffeemaker and has this stuff put in which sits twenty minutes and has to be washed out. This means cleaning the sink.

Somehow this reminded me of the other worst chore, which is defrosting my self-defrosting refrigerator. I have the kind that you scrape frost from with a plastic shovel now and then, more now than then. I found myself scraping away and making up a tune to go with "Life is earnest, life is real, and the grave is NOT the goal." Defrosting took quite a while and then ensued the washing up of the kitchen floor, which had melted ice flakes all over it. By then Holly and Teddy were ready for a run and a snack. The birds were ready for more food too. So I got us all fed.

And I really cannot say how I found myself cleaning out the fireplace cupboard in my room, which is always a horror. It reminds me of a stuffed toy that has had too much use and the slightest touch will send the insides all over the room. I am sure most women organize their storage space; mine just looks after itself. This particular cupboard is lined with the ancient plaster made of sand and hair, and a good deal of it sifts out on the rug when you open the door. So I had to get out my worst enemy, the vacuum cleaner. I am always on the wrong side of the hose and that is only one problem.

At suppertime, I fixed a pickup meal and watched Huntley and Brinkley. And thus ended my day of complete rest, and it had been very wearing! But since I had theoretically rested all day, I felt I should really work at the typewriter a couple of hours. And this involved putting in a new ribbon. I hope changing a typewriter ribbon is just a personal disaster for me, not one in general. I am always covered with ink, and yards of old ribbon have spiraled under the bed, and the new ribbon, resisting to the end, runs backward and stops, leaving extra loops hanging down on the keyboard.

There is no excuse for this, since I have been typing since I was fourteen. My typewriter is my dearest friend and constant companion. If I ever write a note by hand to the family, I get an immediate response. They call me up, is what they do, to ask what I said and why didn't I type it? So it is only the ribbon that is my enemy. Usually I keep using the old one until my son-in-law Curt or Jill's son-in-law Val turns up and I work the conversation around until it seems natural to say, "As long as you are here, would you mind——"

Finally, I went outside to see if I could detect a hint of spring in the air, even at night. It was very still: the smoke from the chimney stood straight up in the air. The moon shed cold silver on the meadow, and I remembered that Hal Borland had told me the Indians had called it the hunger moon. Looking up at it, I thought how fitting the name was, for I hungered for spring, and wide-open roads, and an unfrozen windshield!

I returned to the warmth of my hearth, but soon, worn out by my day of rest, I went to bed, telling myself I would finish *The Blue Lantern* the next day while I ran the clothes washer.

I have learned to plan carefully for week-end guests until mid-March, for sometimes winter prevents their getting here. One February, when my friends Steve and Olive were coming for dinner, I decided a turkey would be nice. As it turned out, they couldn't get down the road, and neither could anyone else, so I had turkey for days and days. There are fifty ways to do things with turkey, and I did them all. The cockers and Holly helped too.

Another time I laid in a roast beef for the children, and my passion for beef was put to a real test. I gave away as much as I could, but even so. . . . I no longer keep the huge freezer going, because I am alone too much of the time to work through it.

Ham is the answer, and I now keep those good canned hams on the shelf all the year round. I baste them with cranberry juice or blanket them with crushed pineapple. Canned sweet potatoes are excellent, and frozen asparagus is easy. Hot bread is no problem, for, if guests do not arrive, the popover mix or muffin mix stays in the box. I always keep cheese and crisp apples and various kinds of crackers (there are so many new ones) on hand. If Jill's grandchildren and mine are due, I buy tons of milk, but if they do not come, I drink some and give the cockers extra bowls of it.

Winter week ends are wonderful for the small folk, provided the roads are clear and their parents can risk the trip from the city. Children have the same relationship with snow that puppies do. They get right down and roll in it, throw handfuls in the air, and eat it. When they are dragged in, soaked and frostbitten, they scream. Perhaps since they are city dwellers the fact that the snow is clean intoxicates them. In the city they are not allowed to set foot in the sooty, rubbish-laden mess. But the snow at Stillmeadow is white as pear-blossom petals and is deep and soft until March. The children lose their mittens and the bunny hoods fall off, and when they come in their small hands are swollen and blue. But no matter, they just give in and scream to go right back out! They do not, no, they do NOT want hot cocoa or a nice piece of white meat of chicken or even a cookie. They want snow. It makes me wish I could give a yardful of snow to every child in the world.

Speaking of children, Muffin, my granddaughter, is now grown up enough to compose songs. My favorite is: "Fair and air! / Fair and air! / Fair and ai-ai-*ai*-ai-air." It makes as much sense as some modern song lyrics or modern verse. Of course, for her song, you must run in circles while singing.

We can learn much from the wisdom of childhood. My friend Lois called out the back door the other day to see what her grandson was doing. He was sitting quietly in the shade with his Teddy bear and the Siamese cat, Mrs. Murphy. When Lois asked what he was doing, he said, "I'm loving, Grandma. Jus' loving." Grownups, alas, often do not take any time out for "jus' loving." Life is so busy, harried, confusing. But we ought not to go through life like express trains.

Some of my happiest memories, for example, are of the afternoons after school when Mama and I had tea and thin slices of toasted poundcake. I never thought of how busy she was, but I know now she did more than any three women I have ever known. Yet she sat quietly listening to me tell about what had happened that particular day, dramatizing everything no end. Sometimes her shining brown eyes might twinkle, but she never criticized. I innocently thought the tea and cake were what mattered, but it was her caring that made those afternoons so full of sunlight.

One of the main problems in our country, to judge by my mail, is of busyness. There is never any time to do what we want to do, says a friend, and I never do catch up. What is wrong?

I've thought a lot about this because busyness doesn't

seem to be connected with wealth or poverty, city or country. I haven't in years known anyone who had real leisure. I should define leisure, for I do not mean just giving up and sinking into a lethargy; I mean time to think, to read, to hear music, to walk in snowy woods, to drop in on a loved friend for no reason at all but to see her. I should, perhaps, call it constructive leisure. I do notice that often illness is connected with what we call so lightly "overdoing."

"She's been overdoing for years," we say righteously, as we rush on overdoing.

It seems to me the body is the house we live in and deserves as much care as we give to the waxing of floors and scouring of ovens. (It must have been fine to be a pioneer and cook always in an iron pot hung over the open fire.) This was brought home to me when I took Holly to the veterinarian for a check-up and medicated bath and to have her teeth cleaned. I got the vitamin pills and so on for her. On the way home I told her if I spent as much time caring for myself as I did for her I might be in as good shape as she was!

She runs a couple of miles, I notice, and then comes in and lies down and rests. Most dogs will exercise violently and then curl up and doze off briefly. For the very young, it may be a five-minute break; for the older, half an hour. The trouble with homemakers is that the minute they decide to sit down and rest those aching feet, the telephone rings or the groceryman is at the door or the children whoop in from school. I can't, of course, solve this national problem, but I think everyone should sit down and draw up a list of absolutely essential daily tasks and another of can-wait jobs. Then a list of all the organizations that demand time and labor. This list should be PRUNED until there is a little leftover time every day. I have some very dear friends who have three children, one parent to care for, two jobs, and work for every worthwhile community cause besides. This includes church, school board, mental health, and so on. The necessary social schedule takes up the slack. They never have an afternoon or evening to sit comfortably and read for pleasure, and they never see the television documentaries—too busy—and they never have time to drop in for a visit with me, despite the fact there are so many things we would love to discuss. We are all, I think, missing something good for the spirit.

I am not in a position to judge, however, for when I became a full-time working writer I gave up bridge with great reluctance. It always came at the wrong time of day and took too much time. Games are a fine relaxation. I've kept on doing jigsaws with Faith Baldwin because those can be left alone or worked on at odd moments. We also do crosswords and play Scrabble. But these are not things to do at a given hour; they are tucked in here and there.

I suspect that some of the fatigue most of us have today comes from the calendar living we do. When my engagement calendar fills up so there is no space left, I begin crossing things off. I need time to turn around in, to watch sunsets, follow the flight of the birds, and just sit and think about the mystery of the universe.

Another contribution to today's nervousness I believe is television commercials. Wives either petulant or actually screaming at their husbands over some kind of detergent, husbands roaring about a household product, children crashing like herds of elephants on fresh floors—these do not make for inner serenity. I could list dozens of commercials that I think add to the pattern of confused living. There are some excellent products on the market I do not buy—being a small voice in a wilderness of profits, I know. But I feel better about it.

Someday the manufacturers may give us a better picture of family living!

Sidonie Coryn

March

THE COLOR OF MARCH in my valley is brown—there are more hues, tints, and tones than I can add up. A wave of pinky brown crests the edges of the swamp, cinnamon grasses stand to their knees in snow-melt, and drifts of reddish-amber leaves lie along the hollows of the old stone fences. The pond is so brown as to be almost onyx. Well, I have to say simply that I wish I could put March on a canvas framed with sunset over the pines.

This month brings a patchwork quilt of weather. One day sleet laces down and fresh icicles hang from the old well house at Stillmeadow. The next day sparkles with sunshine. The old house vibrates as the wind roars down the hills. Sometimes ashes scatter all over the floor as gusts rush down the chimney, and I like to think that the winter weariness is being blown away by the wild wind.

Sometimes a branch crashes outside the window late at night, and I listen to see if anyone is in trouble on the road. People get lost easily in our part of the country. In earlier years, when Jill was alive, she had a kind of rescue mission organized with flashlights, cables, planks, and so on. She really enjoyed hauling someone out of George's brook at midnight. I offer tea and sympathy and a direct phone call to Arzie Bennett.

A few neighbors have the snow tires off their cars. Some will still be using them in May. Wise people go along with the postman. The day I meet him at the mailbox and note he's using plain tires, I go right down to have mine put on.

The cockers and the Irish begin to dig up the yard again, so I know the small inhabitants underneath are stirring from their winter siesta. The skunks, too, are coming out, and I hope fervently they stay out—outside the fence. There are few things so mystifying as hibernation. Why do some animals hibernate and some not? (Why not the weasel, for example? Instead, he changes to white to match the snow and slips along the fences with a gliding motion.)

The Indian name for the March moon was the full worm moon, which doesn't sound poetic but does suggest life stirring again in the earth. April rains bring the worms up toward the surface, and without worms the soil would not be friable. So worm moon it is! But when I look out at night and see a cold moon rising with an attendant star, I can only think how beautiful it is.

On my first trip to the village dump after the road became passable, I found myself trapped in the car: the door by the driver's seat was jammed. I couldn't get to the other door because of the rubbish piled to the ceiling, and I couldn't launch myself into the back seat where Holly was jumping around. I sat and meditated until a man (ah, men) arrived in a truck and came over and practically wrenched the door off. I thought of all the lives that touched the dump, the things once precious and now discarded—as we also discard treasured friendships perhaps, or frayed ideals—the history of our times is written in dumps like mine, and what a time future archaeologists will have. . . . I could picture them with bits of refrigerators (whoever will have those?) and scraps of metal. Well, with all my thinking, I failed to think one sound thought, which was that if I started the car and drove down to Arzie's, he would get me out. I didn't have to sit forever at the dump waiting for a rescuer. The car ran; I was already behind the wheel—certainly I was. But there I sat. Which proves something about my general intelligence better left unproved!

This is the time for end-of-winter menus. I think I like winter food best. I favor pot roasts, savory with vegetables; crispy pork with sage dressing; split-pea soup with ham hocks. My friend Shirley says that in winter she really prefers to cook with the winter vegetables. She and I are traditional in our tastes. And I may say the way she cooks winter vegetables is elegant. My favorite, at the moment, is her Turnips à la Shirley.

She uses 1 large yellow turnip, big enough for four to six servings. She quarters and pares the turnip, then slices the sections in ¼-inch slices. These go in a deep greased casserole in layers, each one sprinkled with a mixture of about 2 teaspoons of brown sugar, plenty of salt and freshly ground pepper, and about ½ of a cup of grated Parmesan cheese. Over the layers she pours 1 can of beef consommé. The casserole goes into a moderate oven (350°) and bakes covered for an hour, then uncovered for another half-hour or until the turnip is fork-tender. I think people who don't like turnips would succumb to this dish, and those who do could make a meal of it.

As a matter of fact, this is a good time to keep the emergency shelf well stocked, for on bright week ends city friends like to come and breathe the country air. A favorite is Sylvia Gibson's Clam Pie, which can be made from canned or fresh clams. The recipe calls for 2 cups of chopped fresh clams or 3 cans (7½ ounces each) of minced clams. Combine the clams with ½ cup of clam liquor, ½ cup of milk, 1 well-beaten egg, ½ cup of cracker crumbs, ¼ teaspoon of salt, and ⅛ teaspoon of pepper. Have ready enough pastry for a 2-crust, 9-inch pie tin. Put the filling in the crust, dot with butter or margarine, add the top crust, and cut a hole in it so that steam can escape. Bake in a very hot oven (450°) for 15 minutes, then at 350° for 25 minutes, or until golden.

I like to serve a green salad with the clam pie and a bowl of fruit and cheese for dessert, with plenty of coffee.

Along about now I begin to have ideas about the storm windows. Perhaps one sure sign of spring coming is the countrywoman's yearning to get the screens back on!

"It's too early, Mrs. T," says Erma, who has to supervise this task. And if I insist, we invariably have the worst blizzard of the year as soon as the screens go on. Meanwhile Erma decides we might as well wash the curtains and have them fresh. The house begins to smell pleasantly of wax, and we both feel we are advancing spring in some way.

It is far too early to spring-clean. All month long the dogs track in mud. As frost comes from the earth, the yard turns into a low sea of it, thick and dark. There is nothing to do but sponge up the worst spots and tell guests not to bother to take off their rubbers, for it does not really matter. It's good clean mud, I always say.

There are plenty of chores to do now, though. I like to clean cupboards now and sort things. For some strange reason, however, I always have more left over than I can put back into the chests of drawers, shelves, or closets. I end with a few cartons full of things I simply have no place for. These go in an upstairs closet; from there they eventually work their way back. When it comes to papers and manuscripts, I begin by making piles of them and end by putting the piles on top of one another in more cartons. Somehow, I think, any house contains many things that have no category and are not fileable. Practically everything I have seems to be this way. I firmly decided, when I was working on *The Stillmeadow Road,* that I would keep the three carbons separated, tucked in separate cartons. This started out so bravely, but then I found I was threading my way around my room between cartons and Holly kept jumping over them and upsetting them. After I unscrambled the pages seven times, I gave up and dropped them all in a sea chest. In a clump!

This is also a good time to sort the spices and herbs and condiments. They do not keep their flavor indefinitely. I think one should date them, but I never do. I open the tops and sniff and let my nose judge. Those that are no longer good go to the dump, and I take my basket to the market and buy fresh. Jill had good luck raising herbs and we dried our own, but now I buy them and think the variety is excellent. I always have a good many mustards, and I now set aside the jars with just a bit of dried mustard in them. I make French dressing and put it in these jars and shake them up, and that saves the mustard and makes a fine dressing.

I use mustard recklessly. I read that in the third century it was supposed to be poison, probably because it made one's eyes weep when it was pounded in a mortar. But by the time of Louis XI it was in favor, and Louis carried his own mustard pot with him when he dined out. He, of course, used Dijon mustard. In the eighteenth century, forty kinds of mustard were available in Paris; ladies were supposed to use the more delicate mustards, leaving the robust ones for the stronger sex! I use four basic mustards, the Dijon, the regular sharp French, the Bahamian (very rich and strong and wonderful with cold meats), and the hot mustard for barbecues. Then I use the powdered English mustard in salad dressings, stews, and some soups. A little of this stirred with vinegar will really make your hair curl.

And then there are seasoned salt and seasoned pepper and garlic salt and onion flakes—and the flavored vinegars. You can make your own by using the herb of your choice and bringing vinegar to a boil, dropping the herb in, and bottling the vinegar. I favor tarragon and basil and mint.

All condiments should be kept away from heat, but mine are right by the range where I can reach them. A long, narrow shelf to the right of the range holds most of them.

I have many thoughts about kitchens. There are too

many wonderful modern appliances for average kitchens to accommodate. I think in the new age kitchens will revolve, and equipment will be layered in the walls. You will stand by the range and push a button, and a whole wall of utensils, electric gadgets, casseroles, and so on will turn slowly before you. Or maybe the old-fashioned pantry will come back.

My cousin Rob and his wife Bebe are in the process of renovating a very old house—well, not so old as Stillmeadow, but within fifty years of it. I fell in love with the pantry; so did Bebe. At one time I used to travel about watching old kitchens being turned into modern dreams. And all at once, when I went into the old house Rob was thinking of buying, I said happily, "And look—there is a pantry!"

How I have changed, I thought. But just consider the countless grills and toasters and rotisseries a pantry will take! Also room for the old bean pot and the iron Dutch oven. True, the pantries I grew up with had about one shelf you could reach comfortably. For the rest, Mama either used a stepladder or knelt on the floor. And what a time it took to spring-clean one! In those days people saved everything: chipped saucers, cups with no handles, cracked plates. You never knew when a broken-tined fork might come in handy.

Bebe and I stood in the doorway of the pantry, discussing the remodeling of the kitchen. Suddenly we both said, "It might be nice to keep the pantry!"

"But you can't have that door opening in your face," said Rob. "Where's my hammer?"

Four minutes later the door vanished to the woodshed.

Then we sat around the big kitchen table and ate home-baked beans and crusty bread and talked about pantries, among other things. We decided the trouble with pantries had been that, because there was no storage space at all in the early kitchens, *everything* was kept in the pantry, so miles were walked—in and out, and out and in. But IF you kept the modern kitchen with its planned cabinets and shelves and then also had a pantry, you would have practically everything a woman could desire.

It seems that everyone who comes to Stillmeadow these chilly days is ready for a stout meal. One especially good dish for a Saturday dinner is pork chops with jellied apple slices. I pan-fry 6 loin chops, core 4 firm red apples, cut them in thick slices, and put them in a large skillet. I dissolve 1 glass of currant jelly in ½ cup of boiling water and pour this over the apples. I cook them over low heat, turning to let them glaze. When they are tender, I arrange them around the chops on a warm platter. Au gratin potatoes and a green salad go well with this dish. For dessert, if any, I have a custard. I do not care for desserts, but this one is light and easy.

A great favorite with the family is baked pork chops and cabbage. I brown the chops, then arrange them in a greased casserole and top them with sliced onions and thinly sliced cabbage. I season this well and pour over just enough milk to cover the mixture. I bake this at 350°, covered, until the cabbage is tender and the chops melting done. It takes about an hour. This dish requires baked potatoes, for the juice is out of this world and you slosh it on the potatoes liberally. It can be prepared ahead of time, too, and tastes even better when reheated. If any juice is left over, it makes a wonderful soup.

Sounds are coming back to our valley now—beginning with the peepers blowing their elfin horns in the swamp and continuing with the redwings and their cool, insistent *okallokalee*. The migratory birds always sound as if they had come home from a safari, but I imagine they sound that way wherever they settle for the winter too. The robins come so early, I worry about them. It always seems to me they start coming in just before a bad blizzard. They live, however. By May they will be bright and sleek. And soon my winter birds will disappear, according to the pattern of nature. I have been told the birds migrate because of light changes, and not weather. Perhaps this explains the arrival of the robins.

One sound I *don't* like is the saw-tooth buzz of the wasps. In an old house like mine there are always wasps, but they don't bother me much until the first sunny days in early spring. Then, going out the back door and past the well house becomes a hazard. I am sure wasps are valuable in the affairs of nature, for everything has a purpose; but I just don't happen to know what wasps do to be valuable. The attic is practically inaccessible any time of year. By the time one climbs up with sprays and weapons, the thing to do is shut the door firmly and go back downstairs for a nice cup of Earl Grey tea.

Bees I like. I enjoy their velvet flight when the first spring flowers come, and I like to think of the pale-gold honey in the comb. Bees amount to something! And they do not go out of their way to sting you.

Occasionally one of the cockers comes in with a lop-sided lip. But Holly never seems to get stung. Her difficulty was with a skunk. I've said before that our own skunks, so to speak, live under the kennel floor and have an arrangement with the dogs so there is never any trouble. Why can't people, I ask the cockers, behave like that? People are queer, they say. However, a nomad skunk came wandering by and Holly investigated. I doused her with tomatoes, according to Dr. George Whitney's recipe, washed her three times, rinsed her four or five, and sprayed her with some of my Christmas White Lilac.

Three weeks later I had occasion to take her to the veterinarian, who said, "Well, somebody I know has had a time with a skunk!"

Wasps or no wasps, the cockers are happy, as if they sense that the season of snow and sleet is over. One way a cocker expresses happiness is to carry something around. Any old stick or scrap of paper will do. Holly prefers to take one of my best boots and vanish with it. I like their philosophy: seek a treasure and cherish it.

"There are two kinds of gossip," said Olive, as we sat by the fire having coffee. "There's the kind like arsenic; some women go around like fly sprays, poisoning the air. You don't believe the gossip, but you can't forget it."

"I know," I said. "Even now, after six years, I remember an untruth about the Aldingtons."

"But just passing along news," Olive went on, "the way that Miss —— does. . . ."

"But it's hard to know where to draw the line," I said. "One kind just fades into the other kind. And have you ever noticed how gossip grows? I don't really need a get-well card because of a cold in my head that suddenly gets to be 'pneumonia'!"

I've noticed that a sure give-away of what I'm about to hear is in this beginning: "Of course, I *never* gossip, but did you know . . . ?"

There is a natural urge to tell things we know, of course, especially if it makes us feel important. But it is generally an expensive indulgence. And there is a way to avoid gossip. I make this test: I ask myself, "Would I like this remark made about me?" If not, it is probably better left unsaid.

Spring garden salads are still far off, but I do like salad, and Ann Wharton's Four Bean Salad is a honey. To make it, drain 1 can of green beans, 1 can of golden wax beans, 1 can of garbanzo beans (or chick peas), and 1 can of red kidney beans (save liquids for soup). Mix well in a large bowl. For dressing, use ½ cup of vinegar (I use wine vinegar), ½ cup of sugar (I skimp on this), ½ cup of salad oil. Slice 1 large onion and 1 large green pepper thin and add to the beans, pour dressing over mixture, and let stand in the refrigerator overnight. Add salt and freshly ground pepper before serving. This is good for a buffet, a nice change from hot beans baked all day. Although to me beans any old way are elegant.

I also feel chicken is basic. I always answer those questionnaires about desert islands with a request for just chicken. Of course I would need things to work with, like a package of cream of leek soup. For one of my favorite dishes, Chicken Special, brown chicken breasts until golden in an electric skillet or the old iron one. For 4 breasts, add 1 package of cream of leek soup with enough top of the milk or light cream to make it of sauce consistency. Simmer away for about 45 minutes (or longer if chicken isn't done), adding more cream or milk if needed. Or dump in 1 can of mushrooms and liquor. (I prefer dark meat, but somehow these recipes come out, even with breasts instead of whole chickens.)

I cannot understand anyone being bored by cooking, because it is always different—there is, I think, no end to the new things possible. I thought I had been exposed to most recipes, having written cookbooks myself, collected them, and begged everyone I ever ate with for just ONE recipe. But last summer I had, for the first time, Bess Clarendon's Appetizers; I ate five. You use ¾ of a large package of cream cheese, 1 egg yolk, grated onion to taste (try 1 teaspoon first) and Accent (monosodium glutomate). Mix well, spread on crackers, and broil. The canapés puff up and turn golden and melt in your mouth.

The moon is full at the end of the month and seems to bring a promise of crocus and scilla and the first daffodil. As the season's cycle moves on, countryfolk move outdoors. Yards are littered with branches; grape vines need pruning and so do fruit trees. Winter mulch is pulled away on a benign day around the time spring officially arrives. It's a good time to burn rubbish, too, for the ground is wet, the trees not leafing. On a clear, sunny day, it's fun to see winter's leftovers blazing away in the garden.

I like to go out in the morning with the cockers and Holly and see what's happening in this world of promise. The snowdrops are up, and surely the lilac buds have swelled overnight. Out toward the old orchard there's a sheltered place where by now daffodils poke green lances toward the sun. Ice melts, the ground thaws, and I stand there sniffing the sweet, clean air. Jill, coming around the corner of the house carrying a shovel or a trowel, used to ask me, "What are you doing?"

"Smelling mud!" I would say ecstatically.

April

THE LOOK OF APRIL at Stillmeadow is
a tentative questioning look. For spring is beginning and yet
winter has not absolutely gone. I note in my journal that the
past five years have brought cold weather, rains, and even
blizzards. But there are days—oh, tender daffodil days! Twilights grow longer, and the air has a different sweetness that
speaks of spring. There are soft moon-deep nights when the
peepers sing sweet in the swamp. The redwings and robins
are back and the juncoes have gone on, following the in-
evitable law of nature. The wild geese go over uttering their
wild lost cry.

The sound of the brook running down the hill is a glad,
free song. The air has a different sweetness, and I wonder
whether swelling buds can have a scent, or do I imagine it?
Of the hyacinths there is no doubt, and I break a stalk of
purple and one of pink to put in the milk-glass spooner.
In May, Stillmeadow will be full of flowers. But the first
ones to appear in April are like young love, a discovery of
the wonder of life. Toward the end of the month hyacinths
and violets bloom, white daffodils open in the Quiet Garden,

79

and the forsythia across the road turns on its golden fountains.

It is time to look for cowslips, and there is only one place I know to find those lustrous golden cups: by the brook where it slips into the swamp. Even if I wanted to, I could not pick them without going up to my waist in icy water. The leaves of the plant are wide and glossy, and somehow cowslips look tropical, which makes them even more of a wonder on a chilly April day.

One blessing for us countryfolk is that the roads are open. In winter I drive with the speed and agility of a snail, and the back-country road seems endless miles of ups and downs. Now, suddenly, it is very short.

Another thing: Muffin can be safely transported from the city for a week end. She is very like April, like a crocus. Somehow she is not a bustling, freewheeling, modern child. She touches things so gently that nothing is broken. She never drops things. Her crying fits are April showers, the sun is out so soon.

She talks rapidly and incessantly in a voice rather like the peepers'. And when she thinks something is funny, she spills over with a chime of merriment. I feel that one reason she dances through the days is that her parents provide a quiet, secure home. If she were overstimulated or pushed, she would certainly be a nervous, jumpy youngster, for she reacts intensely to life. A few years ago Connie, her mother, told me with alarm that Muffin was intent upon learning the alphabet. She just kept at them until they said yes, that was D. I said not to worry. I could read well when I was four, and I don't think it damaged me for life!

There is a lesson here, somewhere, about reading difficulties. If parents read, and books are all around, children just feel an urge to read—and do so. They do it just as children of famous swimmers seem to be born ready to leap into deep water. Circus children swing from the trapeze at an incredible age, and why not? Everyone else in the family is doing it! And farmers' children swing scythes bigger than themselves.

Muffin has an unrelenting interest in my typewriter, which I do not allow even adults to use. I firmly believe that all the words I shall ever write are in my typewriter, and if anything ever broke the spell I would write no more. A typewriter is the essential companion day and night. Sometimes I seem to hear mine sigh as I tear up a dozen pages. Wasting *our* time, it says plainly. Writing is like cooking. I must have made hundreds and hundreds of soufflés, but, as the last bit is consumed, I always wonder whether a pinch of this or that might have added something. I never say so, however, for I believe there is nothing so tiresome as an apologetic woman.

So the typewriter is off limits to Muffin, but I hope to buy her one when she can use it. I wonder whether her passionate love for the typewriter is a forecast of her life.

This is clean-up time. I go outside and collect the empty cans that Holly took out all winter. She loves to carry one around for a while and then deposit it somewhere near the lilacs. It's time, too, for the cockers to get good shampoos and a trim, for soon it will be sunny and warm. My young neighbor Tommy goes about the yard gathering up the small fallen branches for my fireplace. Joe collects the larger ones that came down during the winter storms and cuts enough dead trees to build up the woodpile. At Stillmeadow, the fireplace is seldom empty. "This year," Joe tells me, "you're burning ash and locust and maple—no apple trees fell."

Now that winter is past, countryfolk can be reasonably sure that guests will arrive on time for dinner. Yet nights are still cold enough for the kind of meals I like best. A good supper dish to serve is Quiche Lorraine.

To make it, line a 10-inch pie tin with pastry, prick it with a fork, and chill. You need 1 cup of grated Swiss cheese, 4 eggs slightly beaten, 2 cups of thin cream, a pinch of cayenne pepper, a pinch of sugar, 1 teaspoon of seasoned salt and seasoned pepper (or regular salt and pepper), 1 diced white onion, and 6 or 8 bacon slices.

Beat eggs and cream together until blended; add seasonings and stir. Grill the bacon and break into bits. Sauté the onion in butter or margarine until transparent. Now butter the pastry lightly with soft butter. Sprinkle the bacon on first, then the cheese, and pour the egg mixture over. Bake in a hot oven (450°) for 12 minutes, reduce to medium low (325°), and bake until a knife inserted in the center comes out clean. For most ovens, 25 minutes is enough. This serves four.

Served with fruit salad and coffee, this makes a happy meal. For six persons I make two pies and have none left over. Quiche Lorraine freezes well and is nice to have on hand for unexpected company.

My friend Margaret Stanger, who lives on the Cape, makes a specialty of home-baked-bean suppers. Four or five of us gather, and I shamelessly arrive first so I can park my car near the house. It is set in the woods on a rather steep hill, and I must favor my bad knee. The house is old, almost as old as Stillmeadow, low and slant-roofed. The keeping room is paneled in mellow pine and furnished with Early American pieces. The vivid heavy curtains match the color of the fire on the open hearth. The tablecloth is red too; it came from Italy but is very much at home on Margaret's table.

Dinner is baked beans, in a fine old bean pot, with the juice bubbling over. Rich brown bread goes with the beans, and a green salad with hearts of artichoke. For dessert, real Indian pudding—a dish that few of us know how to make nowadays.

In April rains can be severe. The last downpour a few days ago inundated the woodshed roof and accumulated there. I use the woodshed as a cooler up until May, storing certain food items there, and when I opened the door later that day I felt as if I were under Niagara Falls. I was carrying a pot roast and a big kettle of soup, and fortunately I managed to keep both out of the falling water!

Bob Morrow came over early the next morning and climbed to the woodshed roof, leaving his two small sons to run around the yard and play. It seemed no time at all before the smaller boy had found his way to the pond and fallen in—up to his waist. It set me to wondering why so many children fall into ponds.

The boy's father brought him in the house, and I suggested putting his dripping clothes in the dryer while he was wrapped in a blanket. But the lad drew himself up with admirable dignity.

"I do not want to take off my things," he said.

He wouldn't even take off his shoes.

Although he seemed no bigger than a drenched kitten, he refused to be babied. So I set him on a chair beside the radiator and offered him a glass of milk. He accepted this; also a pad of paper. But not a pencil. Instead, he wanted a pen!

I left him alone for a while, and when I returned he gave me a manly smile, extending one leg.

"My pants is drying," he reported.

Later, we parted with mutual respect. It isn't likely that I shall see him again—unless the roof leaks and I call his father to repair it—for he lives many miles away. But I shall think of him. I suspect that many a member of the very small set would have screamed with fright on falling into the water and, afterward, would have expected all the waiting on in the book. This boy, I think, will make a fine, self-reliant man.

There have been two changes in the house in recent times. Both kitchens were painted and the pine cabinets redone in the middle kitchen. Ed Davis, who did such a superb job, came over with his wife one evening and made some comment on the previous state of the back kitchen.

"Well, guess who painted it last," I said. And admitted I did. That was why it was three colors. I had only painted what I could reach, and there were two former jobs, one by Jill, in the same way. So it was partly pink, partly a kind of Wedgwood blue, and the reachable portions aqua. Having it all one color, two coats, made such a difference that of course it led to new valances and some other things.

Then the antique carriage lamps that we used as door lights for the two front doors finally rusted right out. We had bought them at an auction years ago, and now copies of these old lamps replaced them. I must say the light is better!

And of course America has moved outdoors in the past twenty years, so every spring Erma helps me assemble the lawn furniture. We face a sorry sight: rusted table legs, sagging canvas, torn plastic. We usually begin by making a trip to the dump and then progress to Danbury looking for new pieces. It should be easy to find good lawn furniture, I tell Erma: my wants are modest. Everything must be portable, because it all travels from the cool green shade of the apple tree to the warm, sheltered terrace by the old well where the wisteria climbs and violets bloom. But it must be sturdy. It must support a leaping Irish setter and firmly built cockers and various small fry that jet about. We had at one time a lovely chaise longue—which collapsed under a guest. He was thoroughly entangled with bits and pieces, and it took some time to sort him out from the debris.

Once we ordered put-together-yourself furniture, and summer was almost over before we figured out how to put the legs on so they went in the right direction. The lovely wrought-iron furniture always lures me until I think of painting it every spring. The redwood is charming—and too heavy. In the end, we get more aluminum stack chairs and a lounger, along with a couple of small light metal tables. And by the time the lawn is ready for basking, the weather changes and snow blankets every surface!

There is one part of household management I never succeed at. I stock the shelves with canned goods and packaged products early in winter, when it is easy to get them through the picket gate, across the yard, and into the kitchen. I plan, I always think, very well for this informal siege. But when April arrives and I decide to go over the shelves, I find that I just have not come out even. I did not come out even last year, or the year before. Why do I have six cans of sweet potatoes, seven cans of apricots, and five boxes of curried rice? I cannot make up much of a meal with that combination of ingredients—and where did the things go that would fit in with them? Why are there ten cans of tomato soup and not one solitary can of chowder? And how did the nine boxes of popover mix get there?

Which brings me to a rather alarming idea. I've read all too many articles about food preservation. I rush meat from George's market and fling it into the refrigerator and hesitate to open the door until I get ready to cook it. I watch the eggs to be sure they are fresh from the dairy counter. It has occurred to me that canned goods probably ought to be used up in a short time and never kept over on the shelves. So this season I decided to use everything up fast or give it away. And I do not, now, want a single wonderful recipe for sweet potatoes from anybody.

In my childhood, my father was a great buyer. He never bought a can of anything, he bought a case. It saved money, he said. So Mama had a lot of this using up to do in her day. But I remember she always managed. We never went on a curried-rice and sweet-potato regime. Nor did the icebox hold a dozen leftovers at any given time.

The articles I read do not emphasize one thing that is really important: the items that are very likely to spoil are staples like flour, corn meal, cereal products, and crackers. I buy flour and such in small amounts. Fortunately the manufacturers put up small packages of practically everything—not as romantic as the old bins in the country grocery, but easier to manage.

Holly and the cockers like to help with leftovers except carrots. I am not much on leftover carrots either, so perhaps that is why. I like crisp slivers of raw carrots and carrots in stews and freshly dug baby carrots with peas. The baby carrots also come in cans now, which is a help for anyone without a vegetable patch.

It is wonderful to have as a gift from nature a garden you can cultivate; but there are other gifts too—wild strawberries, which taste sweeter; wild grapes, which make the best jelly; morel mushrooms, which we used to pick in the old apple orchard. The morels have gone, but I keep hoping that they will reappear as mysteriously as they went. These delicious mushrooms are shaped like spongy trees and grow to be as much as two inches high. Sliced lengthwise and broiled in butter, morels are gourmet fare.

Jill's son Don and his family were here one week end not too long ago. Jamie, who has been taking swimming lessons all winter in the city, confided to me that he can do the dead man's float now. Looking up at me through long, dark lashes, he reminds me of his father, and I recall the time he learned to swim at camp. Don had never embraced water in any form, and even with two pairs of water wings he idled at the edge of the swimming hole, not wetting one toe. But the first week end we visited him at camp, he came flying across the sand saying, " I can swim! Watch me!" And swim he did, going through the water like a slim silvery fish.

"Our counselor says there are some people who can't sink," he said as he dripped out, "and I just happen to be one of them!"

Now six feet two, Don has taken up skin-diving while his son learns to float. Tall man, small boy, and the pattern repeats itself. It made me think, as I watched Jamie in his father's lap, that perhaps the real secret of success in life is faith that we cannot sink! When we are faced with a problem, if we believe we can solve it, we are likely to. So, as you embark on a new course, why not assume you cannot fail because you just happen to be one of those who cannot sink!

Spring has a special effect on us in the valley. The whole beautiful world invites us out, and we have an urge to wander. The gentle, rolling hills; the clear, winding brooks; the bright, rushing streams: all are filled with the rhythm of life, and we move with it too.

There are still wild stretches of woodland and mysterious deep swamps. On my own forty acres there are two swamps, which are havens for all kinds of wildlife. Wild cranberries grow in the smaller one, which we call the front swamp. High-bush blueberries fringe the larger or back swamp. Once, in the early days, for some reason we felt we had to cross the back swamp, and we laid long boards across the hummocks. As soon as we stepped on them, board and hummock sank and we sank too, scrambling to safety just in time. A swamp is not meant for people; it belongs to the wild folk, and I wish men who drain swamps would reflect on this.

I don't know how many lakes there are within driving

distance of Stillmeadow. There are nameless ponds too. They look as if a string of blue stars had broken in the sky and fallen at random. The water is usually clear and cold, and since we have no legendary Loch Ness monster or famous alligator these lakes are fine for swimming. My own pond was nine feet deep and held roughly 200,000 gallons of water, but silt has come in from the back swamp for some years and it should be dredged out. But when I think of the fish and frogs and wild ducks who nest at the upper end and the blue heron that comes at dusk, I realize the pond cannot be disturbed.

Steve and Olive have muskrats in their brook, as well as trout, but I have never seen them in my pond. They also have a resident woodchuck—very old, very big—and they actually watched him last fall as he stuffed his mouth with dry leaves from a heaped-up pile and carried them into his burrow. Back and forth he went until he had his winter quarters built to his taste. No doubt some folk would be able to tell how severe a winter to expect by counting the loads of leaves he hauled!

I feed the birds year round but give up the suet as soon as the weather is warm enough to melt it. Many birds love peanut butter, but I was advised some time ago never to give them just plain peanut butter because it sticks to the roof of their mouths. I can well believe it: it sticks to mine too! I hear there is a new unstickable kind but haven't tried it. Meanwhile, a bird expert advised me to always mix peanut butter with seeds, crumbs, or something to keep the stickiness out. I am now worried about the years when I hung juice cans of pure peanut butter out. Once I bought ten big jars of the spread at the store and George, the owner, said he wondered, that was all—just wondered!

Evenings now have a special magic, and I spend many happy hours out of doors. Lovely are the willows in the half-light, all smoky gold with green mist on the branches. We didn't know very much about willows when Jill planted a number of them out by the pond. Once their feet were firmly set in the wet rich soil, those trees grew and grew and *grew*. Now, two of them are tangled together, and when they are in full leaf I can stand under the branches and believe the sky itself is green.

There are not many willows in my valley, and I wonder why. Their long, fountainlike limbs are the most graceful of any tree I've ever seen. Jill had a special love for them, and we used to drive over to the old mill to see some particularly beautiful ones that grew there.

A full pink moon—April's autograph in the sky—shines down over Stillmeadow. Remembering the white gold moon of January, the ball of pale copper at harvest time, June's daffodil eye of night, I ask myself: Who can say which is the most beautiful? Each has its own charm, each bestows its own blessing, and we welcome each in turn. The planet we inhabit may be only one of countless planets, but it turns in its accustomed orbit and we accept this unquestioningly. There is a security in knowing that spring follows winter and summer comes after spring. As I go back into my house, I wish all my friends, everywhere, the joy and sweetness of spring.

Sidonie Coryn

May

THE FIRST TIME I went to the Metropolitan Museum in New York, I was so overcome by the riches that I felt faint. I managed to bear it until I got to the El Greco, and then I sat down trembling, and when I could get up again I went right down to the basement and had a pot of nice ordinary tea and a pedestrian, rather stiff, sandwich. For the truth is there is a limit to how much excitement one human being can endure.

I feel the same way about May, when apple blossoms cloud the air, tulips and narcissi bloom, violets are thick enough to walk on, and the lilacs lean above the white picket fence heavy with fragrance. May would be a wonder, I think, with just one blossoming apple tree or one small white lilac. Or one violet plant with purple blooms and heart-shaped, dark leaves. I would like to be able to play a lute and sit in the dappled shade and sing the hours away. However, I cannot carry a tune and the only instrument I ever could play was the ukulele, except for a brief struggle to master the guitar. So the music just stays in my heart.

It's time to get out the picnic basket and follow the footsteps of spring down the green valley and up the far hills. The tumbling brook, fringed with fern, skips over jeweled stones. The children used to make collections of the smooth ones—rosy, silvery, greenish. We'd take sandwiches and jugs of coffee and milk and sit on a flat gray ledge; while the children waded in the swift water, Jill and I would dream of making a wildflower garden in a smooth place at the brook's bend.

The garden never materialized, for leisure was hard to come by, what with raising all our vegetables, canning and freezing them, mowing a half-acre lawn, and taking care of cocker puppies and, during the war, eighteen laying hens.

I am a great believer in dreaming. Once you feel satisfied that everything is just so, you narrow your horizon. This is a far cry from not enjoying what you have. It just means not being static. Even an unrealized dream may be a blessing.

One of our dreams was realized, but it didn't just happen. There was a desiccated corncrib in the yard when we bought Stillmeadow. It was one-third full of rotting corn. We decided that where the crib stood would make a lovely Quiet Garden. Very simply, too.

First, it took a week to lug out the corn. Then, as we neared the bottom, a thousand mice came skittering out. Jill flew to the house, for mice and snakes scared her more than a pride of lions. The mice tried to move into the house. So we had to have the foundations pointed up. Also a new floor in the kennel to keep the mice from moving in with the cockers. Then we had to hire a man to cut down the main beams because we couldn't lift them. And then we were left with the sorriest mess of rubble and mouse nests you ever saw.

It took days to clean all this up, after which we got a load of flagstones to lay in the middle of the garden and then hired Mr. Clark to put up a picket fence. After that, it took Jill about three years to reclaim the soil, get bulbs started, and plant roses and a lily-of-the-valley bed.

Like most hopeful gardeners, we put in too much, too

close together, so Jill had to spend more time moving things out! But when the day came that we had some cedar furniture in the garden and ate our first lunch under the flowering crab, I said happily, "And to think this didn't cost anything!"

"Just a gift," said Jill. . . .

Lilacs are in bloom; on the old well house, wisteria begins to open amethyst buds. I am dazzled by all I see, but perhaps best of all I like the slope above the pond, where the daffodils and narcissi that Jill planted shine like countless gold and white stars. Again I ask myself, is this the same countryside that only a few months ago was swept by bitter winds? Or did I only imagine the stinging snow and glittering icicles? Changing seasons will forever be a mystery to me. Time has folded winter away into yesterday; tomorrow, summer will make May just a memory.

These are happy days for young Jamie. He has become a collector of bugs, toads, frogs, spiders, newts, snakes, even dead wasps. He'll collect anything that he finds out in the garden or by the pond—and not all of these creatures are welcome additions to the household! I have to step with caution when Jamie announces he's lost his best worm on the stairs. At home they get tired of moving the refrigerator to retrieve a lizard or some other treasured creature.

I believe children show their main traits at an early age, even if they seem to change later. Jamie may become a doctor, like his father, but I suspect he will always be a naturalist at heart.

Of course, at his age, all kinds of ideas come to mind. Just the other day he told me that he'd decided to become an archeologist, so could he dig in the old vegetable garden? "Why not?" I replied.

"Of course," he said, "it's possible I might decide to become something else later on."

I agreed this was possible. So he dug. He was outside two hours and then came in rosy with triumph. "I have found some old bricks," he announced. "They may be antiques."

"Good heavens!" I said, "You've been digging up the leaching part of the septic tank! Get your father."

His father stopped working on the picket gate (which is always in trouble) and went out to relocate the dig. In the end, they went off with several large ominous lumps of what his mother Anne said was caked mud and he said was antique stone.

Jamie also likes to sing. One afternoon as I was resting briefly, a round, earnest face suddenly appeared at the foot of the four-poster. " 'I've been working on the *rail*road,' " he began firmly. He sang it strongly, in a mannish monotone. Then he sang it again. And then again. By the fourth time, I considered suggesting some other tune. But he indicated the concert was over by vanishing into the kitchen to look for a jar to hold more worms (the lost one never turned up).

One thing I have learned from years as a countrywoman: people here love the land. When Jill and I first came to

Stillmeadow, this was farm country. Stillmeadow had been a farm, and the nearest neighbors (not very near) were farmers. The kind of farming would horrify Midwestern farmers, accustomed to a rich expanse of arable soil that you could lay out with a ruler if you wanted to. Here, the soil was all right once you got to it. But first tons of small rocks, big rocks, and boulders had to be painfully grubbed out. As a neighbor put it, "The best crop is always stones."

When a farm has to be sold, it is a sorrowful affair. The farms do not pay and one must live. But where the pre-fab houses go up, we remember.

"Those people live on the Olsen hay meadow," we say. Or, "Yes, that is the Harrisses' woodlot where those houses are going up."

This love of land is not going to die out, I am glad to say. Tommy has already picked out a special parcel of land that will be his when he is grown up. It is, he says, nice land. I find this comforting in a world where so many people rush about seeking new horizons.

The glacier that left the boulders and stony soil also scooped out endless lakes and ponds and left gentle hills to temper the wind. It gave us the green valleys with clear streams winding through them, and gray ledges for lichens to grow on. It left craggy places with caves. In a way, too, our lovely old stone fences are a heritage from the glacier. The early settlers cleared the land and thriftily used the boulders along the boundaries. To me, there is nothing much more satisfying than a gray stone fence climbing a green hill in summer or marking a snowy road in winter.

Some folk plow early, some late. Some plant when the maples are in leaf, some only in the full of the moon (I believe in this myself). The truth is that you cannot hurry nature. If the ground itself is not warmed when the seeds go in, they just stay there like stony pellets. When the earth is mellow, the seeds grow like magic. Jill used to be an early planter just because she could not bear to keep out of the garden one more hour. She was a quiet person, and the only time I heard her sing out loud was when she began planting. She loved the earth itself and used to stand sometimes just holding a handful of it and humming. There was a special communication between her and the earth, which I suspect is the test of the born gardener.

It is interesting to speculate whether we are born with a sense of the beauty of special things or whether early associations establish it. I am passionately fond of violets, but is it because they are more beautiful than many other spring flowers? Or is it because they remind me of walking in greening meadows with my first love and gathering baskets of them? We grew up in a small Wisconsin town with the broad Fox River circling it and rich fertile farmlands stretching to the horizon, and deep woods, and tamarack swamps and lakes, and the usual cliff where an Indian maid leaped to her death for love. (I must say I have never lived anywhere without hearing about the Indian maid or Indian chief who leaped from some cliff or hilltop. The country must have really swarmed with jumping lovers in the early days.)

I am not sure whether the Wisconsin violets were bigger and brighter and sweeter than anywhere else, but they had that special grace of love in springtime. Years later a woman in Williamsburg gave me a peach basket of Confederate violet roots which established themselves happily in Yankee soil. These have large blooms, ivory with blue centers, and they remind me of an idyllic time in Virginia in the gardens of the Governor's Palace.

There are lots of violets at Stillmeadow. I like to go to the upper meadow to find the white ones, which I put in a tiny child's mug. By the back door bloom the almost-black purple ones, which are much larger and have wider shining leaves. I suspect these were planted in that particular spot many years ago. The present kitchen was the former milk room, with an iron sink and hand pump and a long wooden table for the milk jugs. From the window, as she strained the milk and scrubbed the pails, the lady of the house could look out and see the violets, and perhaps she, too, picked bouquets for an ironstone cup. I feel her presence often, for I believe we leave something of ourselves in the houses we have loved and lived in.

There are the regular blue violets too, shorter-stemmed and plentiful in number. They pop up in the middle of the lawn, bloom at the edge of the pond, and grow by the wood-shed where the white lilac is coming out. They have stolen out beyond the fence to carpet the vegetable garden; they peep around the end of the woodpile. In short, they take over!

Meals are easy for me in May. Asparagus is what I eat! I like it on toast for breakfast, as salad for lunch, and for supper with a chop. I cut it just before it is to be cooked, when it is snapping-fresh.

When week-end guests come unexpectedly, the stand-by canned and frozen vegetables are a help. I like Ann Hansen's green beans with Swiss cheese sauce. Melt 1 tablespoon of butter in a small pan, blend in 1 tablespoon of flour, ½ teaspoon each of salt and sugar, and ⅛ teaspoon of pepper. Add ¼ cup of milk, blend well, and cook for a minute. Then remove from the heat and stir in ½ teaspoon of grated onion and ½ cup of sour cream. When this is well blended, mix the sauce with 2 cans (1 pound each) of heated and drained green beans. The small whole ones are best.

Mix with 1½ cups of shredded Swiss cheese and pour into a buttered casserole. Combine ⅓ cup of cornflake crumbs with 2 tablespoons of melted butter and spread on top. Bake in a hot oven (400°) for 20 minutes. This serves four. With sliced ham and hot buttery biscuits, this makes a good supper for casual droppers-in.

What will this summer bring, I wonder? One year I was buried in recipes for a new cookbook. Toward the end of that summer I got so tired of recipes that I lived on boiled eggs and broiled chops. By the time the book was out, I was cooking again, and enjoying it, and collecting more recipes from friends. For there is no such thing as an end to adventures in cooking.

Life with the grandchildren is much less complicated in May than in December! Gone are the snowsuits and boots, hoods and mittens. It takes twenty minutes to garb one small three-year-old in winter, and I get tired just WATCHING the parents struggle with zippers, straps, and buttons. The small one goes outside and half an hour later is back in again, covered with ice and snow, and there go another fifteen minutes getting the sodden clothing off. Now, all that we have to do is open the door!

Only the other day I looked out and saw Don's daughter Betsy rolling on the green grass with the cockers. I noticed that she was feeding them dog biscuits—those pretty colored ones. Holly was not the least interested: she doesn't care for dog biscuits. However, I saw that Betsy was giving a biscuit to each dog and taking one herself. All of them were chewing happily. I have made it a firm practice never to interfere with the raising of the new generation, so I didn't say anything. I reflected that anything more sterilized than a hard-baked dog biscuit could hardly be found. Perhaps she was just trying to be one of the cockers.

Later on, in the house, when her brother Jamie was consuming his fourth banana of the afternoon, Betsy refused one. But she climbed up on the back kitchen counter when nobody was looking and helped herself to more dog biscuits. As she came drifting past me I noticed she had chosen a yellow biscuit which matched her fair hair!

It's obvious that Betsy is never going to give a thought to insects, frogs, or snakes. But she is like Jill in her devotion to dogs. Whenever the family arrives for a week end, we just turn the cockers over to Betsy in the back kitchen and shut the door. There they play safely and happily for an hour or so while we fix a meal or settle down for a chat. Betsy never pokes eyes or pulls ears. She never screeches. She just acts like a friendly puppy, and they adore her.

As I looked out into the driveway one day and spotted Betsy riding alongside Joe on the small tractor, I wished that every child could be brought up in the country, or at least spend plenty of time there. A city has much to offer—museums, theaters, concerts, zoos—but children should be able to dig in the dirt, climb trees, catch frogs, chase butterflies, wade in a brook, pick wildflowers, play games on the clean, sweet grass. What could be better than any one of those things on a bright spring day?

Jonquil recently had to go to Dr. Whitney's to be treated for a kidney ailment. As I sat in the waiting room, I noticed the anxious faces of the people and the generally resigned look of the patients. Most of the people were not what you would call members of "the Four Hundred"; they were tired working folk, some a bit shabby. I was happy to think that in our country there is no caste system where loved animals are concerned. George Whitney came out, gently picked up one of the cats, and asked, "What is her name?"

The weary young man flushed. "Well, she hasn't a real name," he said. "I just call her Kitty."

I reflected that Kitty couldn't care less. She didn't have to be called Sugarplum Fairy or Snow Queen's Delight. She was perfectly happy as Kitty. She was loved!

The next day George called me to report that Jonquil was responding nicely but that she seemed a little depressed. She was fine if someone stood and talked to her. I said that Jonquil had been talked to most of her life. I believe social environment is as important for animals as for people. Anyone who reads *Born Free* by Joy Adamson can understand that Elsa, the fabulous lioness, was simply treated like a personality, not just another creature.

My constant communication with Holly can sometimes be a problem. She never reads my mail, but other than that I have to be careful. Generally I don't try to conceal anything from her, but sometimes, when she beats me to the gate because I just *think aloud* that it may rain (so I'm off to do errands quickly), I do get flustered.

She is like my second self, even though my family has always said I think like a cocker (and I do). Holly, who is one step ahead of me in more ways than one, has now taken to suggesting I let her out in the morning by picking up BOTH bedroom slippers at once and moving resolutely to the door. I have known a lot of slipper-carrying dogs, but never one that figured out they come in pairs!

Not too long ago I was reading Jesse Stuart's book, *Save Every Lamb,* and decided that it deserves a special place in every library. Jesse writes about animals he has known, and nobody can write better about animals, about people, about nature. He writes like a poet (which he is) and also with a rich pure humor as rare as trilliums in my woods. I met him once when we both spoke in West Virginia at one of those book-and-author things. I was tired from the long train trip and something was wrong with my clothes, as usual, and I was nervous in a hall packed with strangers. And then he walked in and sat down at the end of the luncheon table and began to talk in his soft Kentucky voice, and suddenly I felt life was just wonderful!

I do wish I could have known his Blue Tick pig, but my life has been with dogs, cats, rabbits, birds (wild and tame), and brief experiences with tropical fish (they don't give back enough love for me). I knew one pheasant pretty well, the one called Lydia, but she left me when the bird bath fell on her and trapped her underneath. I also became friends with a very special quail named Robert—who lived in a house on the Cape. But there are so many creatures I have never known intimately, and it is a pity.

This month the full flowering moon floats above the horizon, serene and eternal. Its light is translucent and casts shadows delicate as lace. In the rich nighttime scent of lilacs, it has all the mystery and tenderness of young love.

When I go out into the twilight I caution the dogs to be

very quiet so they won't disturb my unicorn. For this is the hour that he comes on silver hoofs from the darkling woods to crop the wild violets by the pond. Often I catch a glimmer of his horn as he bends his slender head, and I hear the whispering sound of drops falling as he drinks at the waterside.

Everyone, I believe, needs some magic in life—something out of the ordinary, something untouched and purely lovely and unsharable. I have my unicorn. This graceful creature has been called "a fabled beast." In myths he represented purity, and at one time it was thought that to look on him was fatal. In the beautiful tapestry series, "The Hunt of the Unicorn," the fabulous animal is in some scenes shown looking wild and desperate. Mine is shy but tranquil, and he is without fear. I do not always see him when I go to look, but he has long companioned me in the twilight.

It is a lovely thing to know a unicorn.

Sidonie Caryn

June

Of COURSE summer officially begins on June 21, at 3:57 A.M., but somehow the seasons seldom go according to the calendar. Nature follows her own plan as the earth turns. Now, as she casts her spell, daisies open their innocent eyes and gaze out across the fields at the roses cascading over fences. Here in New England the daisies are almost as big as the shastas that are sold in city shops. They grow tall, and when I go out to cut the fading lilacs I can see them nodding above the high meadow grass. The typical New England rose is the rambler, and you can see old-fashioned Dorothy Perkins blossoms practically everywhere you look. Even in deserted dooryards and spilling over fallen sheds. I like them better than the fancy hybrid roses that are so elegant and delicate. Ramblers seem to belong with old saltbox houses and quiet villages and casual winding roads.

I still find a few stalks of asparagus in the garden, but the bed needs doing over. Crops involve work, but then most worthwhile things do. Life itself is like a garden that has times of ripening, times of harvest, times of ice and snow.

No garden is ever finished, I've noticed. I used to find Jill standing in the January snow, looking around at the ground. "I'm going to run the rows the long way this time," she'd say, more to herself than to me. "And add some cutting flowers over there toward the pond."

I find myself doing the same thing. Next year I'd like more irises and another wild rambler. The flowering quince should be moved to a better spot, but this is impractical without a bulldozer. I defy anyone to predict how soon a small shoot will turn into a jungle growth!

When we came to Stillmeadow, the yard was a hayfield, the garden was a tangle of weeds and briers. But in June, day lilies began to bloom all over, lifting tawny cornucopias in great profusion. They seemed like a message of hope for us. When Jill tried to separate them, she had so many that she threw some clumps in the swamp and some on her compost heap. They all bloomed riotously the next June. Their vigor is incredible. They even grew under the giant sugar maples, and still do, all these years later. They are lovely in the house, but each bloom lasts just a day, so bouquets of them are not a lazy woman's job. But in a copper jug on an old trestle table, they are very special.

The honeysuckle which blooms on the fence in the back yard is intoxicating. The masses of ivory and gold and green look almost tropical, and, if honeysuckle did not take over everything within reach, people would pay exorbitant prices for it. The flowers don't keep well indoors, but I bring

sprays of them in anyway because their rich scent perfumes
the whole house.

I remember the days before the Japanese beetle when the
Quiet Garden at Stillmeadow glowed with color. Now it
takes hard work to preserve the specimen blooms. There are
a good many remedies for the beetle invasion. But it needs
a concerted effort on the part of a whole state to conquer
any pest.

I have not taken a final stand on the controversy about the use of insecticides. I do think we may poison the birds and eventually ourselves with the wholesale use of pest killers. (I do not care for fallout either.) On the other hand, the balance of nature has already been destroyed. Wildlife retreats before the throughways and developments. The forests, which give life to the land, are laid waste. Water grows scarce. Tankers dump oil waste and decimate the sea birds and fish. And we are also busy invading space— which perhaps in time we might also ruin.

Now we countryfolk are in summer clothes when we gather in the village market. The young and slim wear shorts and blouses and sandals; the older women look like flowers in their bright prints. The men take to light slacks and short-sleeved shirts. It's almost like a party.

But I have trouble with my summer wear. I shop by mail at my favorite shop. I have a catalogue with lovely colored illustrations of two-piece and three-piece outfits and what are called casuals. I fill out my order blank faithfully, wanting that lilac wash-and-wear to go with my good violet sweater. But on the order blank there is a space for second choice. And the second choice is what I get. So my dress is sage green and I haven't a thing to go with it. When I appear at the market, Eleanor Hoxie says, "Well, I never knew you wore green!" I suppose it is a good thing, in a way, for I never willingly wear anything but lilac, seashell pink, and blue. I also buy the same style of dress year in and year out. By appearing in second choice, at least I get a variation!

We have many travelers going through our village, and after the isolation of winter, it is hard to get used to a stream of cars and a marketful of strangers. It reminds me of a man who asked how to tell the natives from summer people.

"The natives are the ones with clothes on," said the Yankee.

I cannot explain why summer people seem to think it is a fine idea to go shopping in bikinis. And most of them are barefoot. Even the men appear in bathing trunks and nothing else. I just have a feeling that in their own home towns they do not shop without having some clothes on. I don't like it at all, for I think it shows a lack of respect for the inhabitants of the places they visit. As far as I'm concerned, nudes belong in oil paintings and not by the roadside.

On Cape Cod, it is even more noticeable because people go directly from swimming to the stores. Wet bathing suits don't make most people glamorous—far from it. It shouldn't be too difficult to pull on one of those charming knee-length skirts and a sleeveless top before doing the main street! I am always impressed and proud of the way these transients are treated. Good manners, are, I feel, a true part of New England. There is never the flick of an eyelash as a buxom matron goes damply by in a bare minimum (and I do mean bare) of garments. I once didn't maintain my reserve. A really beautiful girl came into the drugstore in a bikini that was gold spangles. Her toenails were lacquered gold to match. She carried a cigarette in a gold cigarette holder. And she wore gold earrings. Somehow the earrings seemed too much. I said "Oн!" in too loud a voice.

I think perhaps the cockers and Holly like June best of all. Days are not hot and twilights are pleasant. The lawn is just right for digging and the air is full of birds to bark at. Moonlight nights are full of wonderful scents and mysterious sounds. Also, I stay out of doors more, and the boy comes to mow the lawn and toss things for them, and week ends the children play games with them. Life is just one long social occasion.

Holly stays out until the first stars prick the velvet sky, but Teddy comes in at dusk because he is always hungry—as a cocker naturally is. The minute the light goes on in the kitchen, he decides it is time to come in and help. I am always reminded that he didn't like the nursing bottle. He didn't care whether he was one of eight (which is too many for a cocker mother) or not. He didn't want a bottle, and the only way he was persuaded to eat was if he were turned upside down. We called him our upside-down puppy for a long time. Now he will almost eat a tin pan!

Holly's favorite job is helping hang out the laundry, especially in this mild weather. There is always a sock or two that gets dropped, and she pounces on it and carries it off and tosses it in the air. That's why there are so many unmatched socks at Stillmeadow! Odd ones turn up under the mock orange bush or in the stone wall or in the wisteria.

Holly has not lost them; she has merely put them away.

Holly has one habit none of the others has. If she wants to go out, she asks politely first. If I say, "Just let me finish this sentence," she eyes me briefly, then utters a firm bark. It is a special bark, reasonable and muted. Then she brings me a slipper and bangs it against my knee. Of course she gets let out!

If she decides to go out at night (full moon) she nuzzles me, at the same time thumping her tail against the side of the bed. This thumping shakes the bed. Next she leans on the bed, putting both forepaws on my arm and pressing down firmly. If that doesn't work, she picks up my slipper and taps it against me, slowly at first, then faster and faster. She precedes me to the door, presenting me with my slipper at the threshold. I stand at the door and watch her pause by the well house, turning her head as she air-scents. Then she is off in the white light of the moon, tail a banner behind her. It takes her usually twenty minutes to complete her rounds, and then she barks at the door and dashes in and in five minutes is fast asleep.

Most of us probably envy the way a dog can drop off to sleep and wake in an instant, ready to go ahead full steam. Holly thinks I am very slow getting up, and I am. I am an off-and-on kind of sleeper, but when I am really asleep, I feel about waking the way I feel about an earthquake. People that bound up singing like larks are a mystery to me. I advance on the day cautiously, as if it might break. I waste a lot of good time just getting started, which time I make up, of course, at the end of the day. I think we humans are engaged in a lifelong battle with time. We rush, we race the clock, we budget the minutes—and somehow we never, never catch up!

It's amazing how the dogs sense when guests are about to leave. Holly begins to look downcast before a single suitcase appears. She never goes to the gate to say good-by, but the cockers do, and then they lean against the fence, peering sadly at the car as it climbs the hill. I don't blame them for being sad: the silence after people leave is very loud. A recent week end was typical. Helen, Vicky, and Janet were visiting me, and as they were going Helen said that the penance for happy hours is the sadness that follows. I knew what she meant.

Sometimes people ask me what we do in the country. Well, Helen and Janet and Vicky can tell you. We all helped Henry put angle irons on my bed, which was gradually collapsing! (Henry Read is one of the most interesting men in the valley, for he knows everything about antiques. A chat with him is like going to the American Wing of New York's Metropolitan Museum of Art.) We all had a wonderful time, flying around, heaving the box spring up, hauling the mattress out, piling the bedding. This is an old rope bed, meaning the holes for the ropes are still in the frame. It is a semi-four-poster, hard maple with tiger maple for the top of headboard and footboard.

While Janet handed bolts and screws to Henry, he reminisced, and I felt I could make a book out of the afternoon. The side rails of my bed are as hard as concrete, and they smoked when he drilled holes for the angle irons. When he stopped to let the wood cool, he said, "I know this bed! I remember it well. How did you get it?"

So I told him—and all at once I began to think of the bed as a person with a history; this is the secret of my passion for antiques. Store-bought furniture is beautiful and charming, but I know there is no life story back of it. With my bed there are countless stories, and if I do not know those who have owned it I can think of them and wonder about them.

It is interesting to consider how antiques reflect the times. Full-size beds in the Colonial period were what we now call three-quarter beds, for people were not so big then. George Washington was a kind of miracle in many ways, and one was that he was six feet tall. I know a good many six-footers. As life has eased and diet has become varied, we have grown taller as a people. We are healthier and live longer. My so-called double bed would not comfortably accommodate two people, although it does very well for an Irish setter and a cocker or so. Plus a stack of books for my night reading, and a bevy of pillows. And, well, it is lovely to look at when the June moonlight falls on the pineapple posts.

There is an old house in Freeport, Illinois, that I used to visit. It is now a museum. Recently my friend Ruth wrote that workmen had found in the cupola a penciled inscription on a narrow strip of wall. It reads:

GEORGE W. BRADLEY, SECOND LIEUT., ELLIS
RIFLES, JUNE 17, 1861. GONE TO THE WARS.
KILLED JUNE 9, 1863. NEAR VICKSBURG.

To me, there is a story here. Perhaps the record was written by a girl who could not marry Lieutenant Bradley. Possibly she was not allowed to speak of him. So she climbed to the cupola and wrote down her heart's sorrow where Father would not know. I hope it comforted her.

When the children come for week ends, I know I must stock up on frankfurters and chopped beef. Sometimes I think the new generation is founded primarily on frank- furters and hamburgers, but since they all seem healthy, it must be a good diet. They do eat a lot of fruit, and they eat green beans and noodles. And that, my friends, is about it.

Betsy, however, will eat anything on a plate. And my own small Anne devoured, at nine months, most of a cheese sandwich left on the table while Connie answered the phone. So there is hope! Betsy eats the way Jill and I ate when we were growing up. Pickles and olives and such things had to be hidden. I loved vinegar, which was not on my diet at all. Sour cream sauce for cucumbers too. Betsy adds salt to her loves. She can turn a saltcellar upside down and pour salt on her minute palm and lap it up like a fawn at a deer lick. She is a joy to cook for now, and I foresee a life of garlic, curry, chili, and other things that make eating fun!

JUNE

The grandchildren love picnics; but grownups do too. And this is picnic time as well as picnic country. There are many roadside spots, with tables and benches and stone fireplaces, to choose from. They all have lovely sounding names like Maple Rest or White Oak or even Frog Rock. After a trip to the market, where buns and rolls, frankfurters and hamburgers flow across the counters in endless waves, you pack the basket with all the favorite picnic foods you can think of. Then all you need do is drive down any country road and stop by a nameless bubbling brook and unpack the basket. There are woodsy places and countless lakes and ponds and hilltops with rolling countryside spread below. There are deserted pastures with gray rock ledges outcropping. I doubt whether in a whole lifetime you could picnic in all of the lovely spots.

One of my favorite picnic treats is charcoal-broiled hamburgers with Louella's Goop. That's what Louella calls it, and every summer I get more letters than Perry Como does, asking for that recipe. To make the Goop, you put ¼ pound of bleu cheese through a sieve. You cream ½ cup of soft butter with ½ clove of crushed garlic. Add 2 tablespoons of prepared mustard, and then salt and pepper to taste. Blend cheese and butter mixture and spoon over hamburgers or steak. It melts into a smooth, delectable sauce. There is nothing like it. It can be done in a blender if you have one.

Wild strawberries are ripening in the meadow, and it's time to pick them (be sure to line your basket with leaves) and carry them home for tea. Strawberry shortcake comes into its own now. There is only one true shortcake. It is not a cake, not a sponge, and this is how to make it:

Sift together 2 cups of flour, 4 teaspoons of baking powder, ½ teaspoon of salt, 2 teaspoons of sugar. I work in ⅓ cup of butter and gradually add ¾ cup of milk. I toss the mixture on a floured board, patting it rather than rolling it. I bake it in a deep pie pan in a hot oven (425°) for about 25 to 30 minutes, then split it and butter both halves. Meanwhile the berries, slightly crushed, stand in a bowl at the back of the range to warm enough to bring out the rich juicy flavor.

I pour the berries on the bottom layer of the shortcake, pour more on top, and serve immediately—with a pitcher of heavy sweet cream. Not whipped cream. This will probably serve four, unless they are dedicated! This dessert is perfect for a June supper. I like it served in shallow soup plates so the juice is easy to spoon up.

The giant sugar maples spread a bright green canopy over the lawn and over the roof of Stillmeadow. When I go out in the morning and look up, it seems to me they touch the sky. I reflect that nobody owns a tree, but a tree graciously accepts all the care you can give. During the February thaw, two lithe young men came over and walked around the yard with Joe and me discussing the health of these trees. It was almost like going to a clinic.

"That one is healthy," said Bob Overton, "but the one next looks sick. And the cables are loose. The one by the picket fence isn't in such good shape."

"I just thought those branches that are leaning on the main cable to the house ought to be taken out," I offered.

"That's your telephone line," said Bob cheerfully.

"She might need the telephone," said Joe.

Ben Savage was prying loose bark from the sick tree. "Needs feeding," he said. "We'll be over next week."

These trees are not only a glory but a heritage from the first owner who put the seedlings in, around 1700 or so. I imagine that he built the house while the family lived in a cabin by the brook. We found the stones marking the site. When I think of hand-hewing all the beams, hand-shaping the clapboards, sawing the wide floor boards, I wonder that he cared about trees. Perhaps his wife said on a boiling August day that she wished she had some shade. So he set the maples all around the house, and naturally he didn't know that in two hundred years they would overhang the roof. I can imagine how he would have laughed as he plunged a hot poker (loggerhead to me) in his hard cider at the thought of those trees ever being fed! But now they are my responsibility, and they get pruned and fed.

Tree men are very special people. They are hard-muscled, slim-hipped, and weathered. They speak of a tree as if it were a person. As they fling a rope into a tree crotch and begin to squirrel into the air, they have a happy look. And from the top of my trees, they must see all the valley and on to the faint blue of the Litchfield Hills.

It seems more rewarding to me to save trees than bulldoze them down.

School is over. The big yellow buses no longer come down Jeremy Swamp Road, and children feel the wonderful excitement of freedom. Tommy finds everything easy except spelling and grammar, and this past winter I think I bored him with daily spelling lessons. It got so he would bound in the house chanting "A-c-q-u-a-i-n-t" or "R-e-c-o-m-m-e-n-d." It had an odd effect on me; I began spelling to myself all the words in my vocabulary! I think we should take a long look at teaching in elementary-school grades. In this age of science, education has progressed marvelously, but after all, words are basic tools and we do live with sentences all our lives. As far as I can gather, we haven't made much progress in enlarging the horizon of the very young with regard to English.

There have been many changes in education. Jill's grandchildren and mine had to be tested for nursery school. Anne enjoyed the tests; she liked playing all those nice games. But Muffin, now safely IN, was frightened by the whole thing. They live in the city; but even so, I wish parents didn't have to begin worrying about education until college. In my day, we just went to school when we were the right age.

Life for children is one big experiment, and they attack it with zest. I wish we could keep our sense of wonder all our lives. I think we take too much for granted, and no doubt this helps us to get our work done, whatever it may be; but I believe an hour looking at a Silver Moon rambler is a well-spent and exciting hour. It is important for me to sit in the leafy shade, and think long, slow thoughts about unanswerable questions, and find serenity. Like the opening bud on the rosebush, a new response to life unfolds.

June twilights are tender and luminous. The grass is dewy, velvet-soft; a cool breath comes from the pines. The cockers cruise amiably nearby as I stroll on the lawn, while the Irish digs one more hole where a mole might pass by. I breathe the rose-sweet air and wait for the moon to rise.

It is so still I can almost feel the slow turning of the earth as it keeps in its eternal orbit. I think of the words in the Bible, "And God said 'Let the waters under the heavens be gathered together into one place and let the dry land appear.' And it was so. God called the dry land Earth and the waters that were gathered together he called Seas. And God saw that it was good."

The infinite wonder of the universe remains. The perfection of a June day is God-given.

July

JULY comes to Stillmeadow clad in silk-blue dawns, blazing gold noons, and violet dusks. Heat glazes the air, leaves droop, and the pond level begins to drop. But night is lovely as a dream, and we can go outdoors without a sweater. Sitting in the garden is inadvisable because the mosquitoes and gnats are busy, but a brief walk is possible.

The hammock swings in the apple-tree shade. The smell of new-cut hay fills the air and cicadas sing. Summer is at high tide now. Elderberries bloom along the country roadside. The clusters of blossoms are pearl-white; later the deep purple berries really ask for picking. Bees feast on the flowers, birds love the berries, and the elderberry bushes themselves are so elegant I wonder why they are not used in gardens as ornamental shrubs. For me in the country, they are a free-and-easy gift of nature.

The cockers move around the house now, following the shade. Jonquil has a lovely cave under the pyracantha bush, which is one reason it doesn't grow much. From there she progresses to the violet bed, and toward dusk she is a blob of gold beneath the Persian lilac. Teddy just seeks the cool stone under the well-house roof.

Holly *likes* heat and stretches out in the blazing sun. When she comes in, her fur is hot to touch. She must have special insulation, for she does not get thirsty, while the cockers empty the water bowl as fast as I fill it up. And I watch it, for there is nothing more heartbreaking than to drive along a road and see dogs chained up in full sun with an adjacent water dish licked dry. Cool, fresh water is imperative, especially these very hot days.

In the evening Holly prefers to wander in the moonlight, but Teddy likes to watch TV. He sits firmly in front of the set, head cocked, forepaws solid, tail wagging. HE doesn't mind reruns, but I do. I think the producers fail to realize that people have more leisure in summer and the audience is a big one and willing. When a new, fresh program comes on, I sigh, because I know it will be replaced by a copy of a copy of another of those situation comedies where husbands and wives try to be attractive while fighting. Plus ten commercials, nine of which should be banned. A commercial can be informative about new products without a knight in armor charging across the screen. And I never buy pills recommended by showing stomach linings. From time to time there are some excellent ones, such as the gum ad with a charming couple dancing a bit and then boarding a ship. I don't chew gum, but if I did, I would buy that brand because the commercial is so attractive. I find I can do a lot of crossword puzzles just avoiding the objectionable commercials.

This is a month of violent thunderstorms. I always begin to feel tense when the air gets heavy and threatening. Then the fierce white lightning scissors the sky and black clouds empty tons of rain on the hot earth as the thunder roars and rolls around overhead. Father would go outside, so he wouldn't miss any of the splendor of the storm. He was what I call a storm buff, but no matter how hard he tried to persuade me to enjoy them too, I never learned to care for them. However, they do break the heat, and the brief presence of pure cool air, sparkling-wet leaves, and lucent sky refreshes the earth.

Fears seem to be instinctive, although some experts say there is a reason, buried deep within us, for any fear. Why then does Teddy panic at the first rumble of thunder and hide under my bed, while Holly leaps to the window sill to watch the storm with interest? Both were raised exactly the same way.

My personal fear is of spiders, large black ones with lots of long legs. Recently, while Don and his family were visiting, we were peacefully eating supper when a huge spider appeared on the wall by the trestle table. Don rose to deal with it, casting an anxious glance at me.

"Why did you go and kill that spider?" asked Jamie.

"Because we didn't have a jar handy to put him in," said his mother calmly.

How I admired her! She did not say that one peculiar adult couldn't stand big spiders. She made it sound circumstantial, and Jamie was satisfied. I decided the next one would be ignored at any cost. However, I reminded myself he didn't exactly need that spider. He already has more than he can keep track of.

Even in hot weather, salads and cold meats get tiresome, and when guests drop in for supper I like to serve a dish that my friend Marie Hinz told me about. It's called Golden Shrimp Casserole. To make it, you use 8 slices of slightly dry bread, trimmed, buttered, and cubed (about 5 cups). Half of this bread goes into a baking dish about 11 by 7 by 1½ inches. Add 2 cups of cooked fresh shrimp (or two 7-ounce packages of frozen, shelled, deveined cooked shrimp), one 3-ounce can of mushrooms (drained), and ¼ pound of grated sharp American cheese. The remaining bread and another ¼ pound of grated cheese go on top of the casserole. Then beat 3 eggs, ½ teaspoon of salt, ½ teaspoon of dry mustard, a dash each of paprika and pepper. Add 2 cups of milk to the eggs and pour over the casserole. Bake for about 45 minutes in a 325° oven, until mixture is set. The dish serves six to eight.

With a green salad, iced coffee, and fruit, this casserole makes a perfect meal.

One of the best things about July is squash. I think the reason some people dislike this vegetable is that they have never eaten it very young and butter-tender, sliced and dipped in seasoned flour and sautéed briefly. Zucchini is delicious sliced and baked in a casserole with alternating layers of tomatoes. Some cooks overcook squash in too much water. It can be steamed in a very small amount of water or chicken broth, barely enough to keep the pan from getting gummed up. It is a good idea to cook diced onion in butter or margarine in the pan, then add the water or broth and the squash. Then add more butter or margarine and plenty of seasoned salt and pepper. Since this is a delicate vegetable, it goes well with thin-sliced sugar-cured ham or peppery country sausage, but I like it with almost anything except pie.

There is nothing comparable to new-picked vegetables, cooked quickly with the right seasoning and butter. And nothing, I must add, that costs more and involves more work. Once Jill figured out that radishes we grew represented about five dollars apiece. But sliced thin and laid gently on warm slices of bread and butter, they were worth it. The Vaneks bring cartons of fresh beets, carrots, tomatoes, sweet corn, and green peppers, as well as squash. One of the nicest things about country living is the sharing that goes on. Ethel Bennett brings jars of relish, pickles, preserves. And Wilma Phillips sends over by Tommy frozen rutabagas and sweet peppers to pop into my freezer. I fare well!

It is now that the habits of city folk appear as a threat. The problem in Southbury is water. We all have wells—a few artesian, most of them just good old dug wells. The water is pure, snow-cool, and clear. Last week a small city visitor said to me, "Gladys, haven't you any water in the icebox?"

"Why?" I said. "Why should I put water in the icebox?"

Then I remember my own city days with tepid water flowing from the tap. I also, in those days, kept water in the icebox!

We also have septic tanks. Now even the stoutest and most willing septic tank will not hold an endless amount of water. We never have any trouble with them until summer guests come. Because we TURN OFF the water when we are not really using it. We do not turn on the kitchen faucet and then go outdoors and play games. We draw the water we need and then turn it off. But this is contrary to the practice of city dwellers and may be one reason why cities have acute shortages in dry seasons.

It does no good to suggest that the well may run dry and the tank "go off." The only way to manage is to sneak around after guests and turn the water off when they are not looking. Fortunately I hear like a hound and I can be in one end of the house and hear the faucet running in the back kitchen. I try to be patient and it is a trial. But after five minutes, I just happen to go to the back kitchen. And here is a most curious fact. Once I get the faucet off, guests rarely notice it. They are so used to running water in the city that they assume it is running here.

Country plumbing is not as tough as city plumbing either. I am resigned to calling Ed Koch at the end of a week end and saying, "Bathroom again." Cigarette butts, stuffed toys, extra tissues, and scraps of this and that do not get digested in my plumbing. What they do is, they stop things up, and water cascades into my dressing room, which is right under the bathroom, alas.

Nevertheless, it is a wonderful time of year when the house is full and really comes alive. The excitement of cars drawing up and children tumbling out and grownups staggering in with luggage and everyone talking at once and the juicy kisses of the small ones (they drink orange juice in the car)—these are priceless. And since the children who visit most often are Jill's and mine, and city-pent most of the time, it is a joy just to see how lovely it is for them to run in clean grass.

Anne finds anything and everything exciting, and she flies around the house, falling down on the waxed floors every few minutes. When she tumbles, tears roll down her pixie face, but only briefly; then she picks herself up, saying, "Ho-kay." I feel sure she will take all the bumps life gives her with the same spirit.

She is also a loving child. I watch her put a very dirty toy rabbit to bed on my sofa with a shabby blanket, her small petal-like hands folding and patting. Then she tenderly lays a dog biscuit beside him. "Just in case you need it," she says gently. "Ho-kay?"

In the evening, after the small ones are tucked in bed with various stuffed toys, the adults sit up and talk, and around midnight Dorothy brings in a snack—paper-thin cold ham, Port Salut cheese, and crusty bread (she baked it herself).

"And what is your opinion of Katherine Anne Porter?" she asks as she sets down the tray.

Which is good for a long conversation!

July, for me, is not a time for projects. I dreamily put off until autumn everything that should be done. I admire my friends who play tennis, go on hikes, and do all kinds of things. Some people seem energized by heat. Jill was one of them. But not I. I suspect that, just as there are day people and night people, there may also be cold-weather people and hot-weather ones.

It used to be very hot in Wisconsin in July when I was

growing up, and I remember the only times my mother ever gave out was when the temperature was around 90 degrees. She would be over the stove with heat waves rising around her, and all at once she would turn a kind of purple-red and feel dizzy. She had to sit down and be fanned with the palm-leaf fan. I used to come in after playing tennis or riding my bicycle, and it seemed to me the look she gave me was bitter. I know why, now.

I believe that as we grow older we understand many things about parents. I can interpret many of the curious activities of my father which seemed mad at the time. It was his urge to create something spectacular that made him almost kill himself building a dock at Ephraim, the dock called Bagg's Folly. I now know how it would seem to wrest ancient rocks from buried depths and make something of them. And be different! I find myself looking at the brook that runs ferny down the hill and imagining myself *changing* its course so it would run by the big gray rock instead of into the swamp!

I also understand more about other people. I really used to nag Jill because she seldom would eat a proper breakfast. Last winter, after a virus, I had a lingering cough. And my breakfast was tea and toast. I mentally apologized to her for never thinking her asthma cough was bad in the morning. I hope I shall never make judgments again about other people. Because how do I know, really, about anyone except myself? Most of us go through life dispensing judgments as if we had a corner on wisdom. "Of course she never should have done that," we say smugly. Or, "I could have told her——" Or, "It seems to me she should have sense enough——" But the Bible says, "Judge not, lest ye be judged."

Midsummer, in fact, is a good time to think about values, for the earth is fulfilling the promise of spring. I reflect that growth comes from the secret life of seed and bulb. And "as ye sow, so shall ye reap" seems a new truth. Some of the hopes I had in spring did not, of course, come to blossom. Perhaps I did not tend them well enough, or perhaps they were not suitable to the climate of my life. But some hopes came to fruition, some plans were completed, and another season I can begin again!

We are all gardeners, whether we plant our rows with love and friendship, courage and honesty, and faith in God —or with intolerance, suspicion, and hate.

My dear friends Helen, Vicky, and Janet wrote, after visiting me recently, that they miss me and Holly so much. "But," added Helen, "we can still 'see' you and Stillmeadow. It is amazing how far you can see when you look with your heart."

Now that the farms are being sold off, I miss the haying time. When we first came to Stillmeadow, hay wagons came down the winding roads at dusk, smelling of summer. By lantern light, farmers would still be forking the last loads into silos. A farmer moves effortlessly; as he bends and lifts the golden weight he is just plain beautiful. I know there is a poetry in the mechanized farming of the Middle West and Far West, but I haven't been intimate with vast harvesting. All I know well is the one-man farm, where the land runs up and down hill and is rocky and resistant. Acreage is always small, and a single barn houses the few cattle. But the New England farmer has few equals for industry, integrity, and independence, and I am sad to see the end of his era. In fact, I am stubbornly preserving my one arable acreage above the swamp and one remaining farmer grows hay on it. He limes the land, plows it, seeds it to good grass, and cuts the hay, and this gives me the greatest satisfaction.

It makes me sad that we are no longer a people who build and plant for generations ahead. With few exceptions, we seem to be nomadic in habit. America is on the move indeed and not always toward progress. Not too long ago I had a letter from a woman who lives in the house in which she was born and married and raised her children. Now the grandchildren come and fill it with laughter. It came to me that this is a very fortunate woman, and I hope nobody ever decides to put a throughway on that land.

Nature replenishes herself unless man interferes. It was man who made the dust bowl. As I read Stewart Udall's book *The Quiet Crisis*, I wished it were required reading for every American. It is a beautiful book, although parts of it are heartbreaking. It may be that no country in the world has such varied natural beauty and such a wealth of rivers, lakes, mountains, plains, and forests. But we have been busy destroying it since we first took it from the Indians. It is time, now, today—not in fifty years when it will be too late—to realize we must conserve every resource. The quick dollars we acquire ruining the land will not feed our children and their children.

On my land, I notice the young maples are coming along. In my time, they will be taken care of so that when the giants finally go, a new growth will be there. When the hurricanes took down the ancient apple trees, we planted more and also put in pines and Chinese chestnuts (which resist the chestnut blight) and started autumn olive along the brook and pond. The result is that the house is set in heavily wooded land where nature can go about her work undisturbed.

The flower gardens in my valley are chiefly informal, set by split-rail fences or along the wandering brooks. They have a casual look, as if the flowers just happened to bloom there. Hollyhocks blossom in dooryards, tall and elegant. They do not, alas, bloom at Stillmeadow, for every effort we made over the years resulted in flat failure. It is better to work with nature than against her, so we planted delphiniums and Canterbury bells, which grow like magic, and Nicotiana, which tends to take over the whole garden. When I go out to pick a bouquet of white and purple petunias, I think how faithful and friendly they are. They ask so little and bloom steadily. There are many fancy varieties, but for me just plain old-fashioned petunias massed in a milk-glass spooner are handsome enough. To me they symbolize a precious kind of friendship—warm, easy, dependable.

Most of us are born with an urge to communicate with our fellow beings. We want to share our thoughts and emotions and, of course, be understood. And sometimes we talk too much, as if we were afraid of silence.

One never knows why a man chooses to lead a solitary life. It always remains a mystery, for such a man never confides in anyone. We used to buy raspberries from a hermit who lives in a tiny shack down the road. Some people call him the honey man, for he also has hives along one side of the plot of land beyond the shack. We once bought strawberry plants from him, and it took some time to persuade him that we could take proper care of them.

"They'll just die on you," he said.

My friend Dorothy Snow remembers when he lost his hound and walked to the village to see if anyone had seen it.

"It has a spot here and a spot or two there," he said, "about a dog and a half long and half a dog high." I think that sentence about the dog must have been the longest utterance our hermit ever made.

Perhaps, after all, our best thoughts come when we are alone. It is good to listen, not to voices but to the wind blowing, to the brook running cool over polished stones, to bees drowsy with the weight of pollen. If we attend to the music of the earth, we reach serenity. And then, in some unexplained way, we share some of it with others.

When the full hot moon makes shadows on the lawn, I forget the breathless, unendurable day. On such nights we used to say in the Midwest that we could hear the corn grow. According to the *Almanac,* Noah sent the dove forth at this time. This bird has become a symbol of hope and peace, and I wish I could send forth a flight of doves to take these gifts to all the troubled people of the earth. Since I cannot, I send my thoughts and pray, "May peace be with us in the days to come."

August

CORN stands silken in the field, chicory stars the roadside, and goldenrod mints her coin. The kitchen smells of spices and syrups, mint and sweet pepper. It is the time of "putting up," a rewarding time for country-folk. I believe it is an instinct in man to store things against the winter, even when there is a supermarket a few blocks or miles away. It is part of the rhythm of life. City people, I have noticed, have the same rhythm. They get ready to move to another apartment or do over the one they cannot move from. They often buy a lot of things, as if they subconsciously felt they had to get ready for something. Sometimes a city friend of mine says, "I really have so much to do to get ready for winter," as she moves restlessly about the kitchen where I am stirring the chili sauce, "I am nearly out of my mind."

But it is only the rhythm of nature working in her, for all of the things she had to do could be done any day, any week, all year round. But in the country, when the vegetables ripen, that is the only time to process them. They set the schedule and nobody can disregard it. I well remember the time we had a bushel of peaches to put up and felt we just had to go to a dog show in Goshen or Ox Ridge instead. From that bushel, we saved just enough for a few small jars of peach butter. One day made the difference.

August used to be a backbreaking time for Jill and me. The house was full of children, guests, and assorted puppies and cats. Still, we managed to can, preserve, and freeze quantities of vegetables and fruits. As far as I am concerned, this kind of work is for two to do together. Conversation is wonderful as you french a dishpanful of string beans or husk a bushel of corn. I think some of the women I know who hate housework basically just don't like to be alone. They will knock themselves out doing all kinds of tedious jobs in organizations, yes. For these they do with someone.

(In the long-gone days when help was easy to get, there was much companionship between the mistress and the household help. On days when my mother's cleaning woman, Mrs. Novak, came, the house was merry with laughter, and the two women often managed to be working in the same room at the same time. At intervals they'd stop for tea. It occurred to me that today neighbors might form a housework association and share the worst household jobs. It is an idea anyway.)

In recent summers Jill's two older grandchildren have gone to camp, and of course they learn all kinds of skills they wouldn't learn on the farm. The programs amaze me because when I went to camp we just swam and canoed and sang around a smoky fire. There wasn't much organization. We got fed and someone looked out to see we weren't drowning! In school, we learned out of books. We didn't have dramatics until high school. But David had a part in a play last winter, based on an Irish folk tale. He was a tree. He was supposed to wear a green shirt and brown pants.

"You'll have to wear your gray pants," said his mother firmly. "You don't have any brown."

"But what'll I say when they ask me why I haven't got on brown pants?"

"Just tell them you are a silver birch," suggested Dorothy.

So the silver birch was added to the production and the play went on!

When I was a small child, I used to visit my grandfather in the summer. He had a farm in West Springfield, Massachusetts, and my cousins and I had wonderful times together. There is something exciting about a stand of corn; I remember how we used to run up and down the ripening rows in a state of bliss. Later, in Wisconsin, I hunted Indian arrows with Father in the cornfields, walking behind him in the golden-green light and scooping up handfuls of rich, springy earth to find tiny quartz bird arrows and shards of pottery.

Still later, my first love and I went canoeing downriver, beached the canoe in a ferny spot, and roasted plain ordinary field corn over a smoky fire. That corn was flavorless and tough, but not to us. It was the rising petal moon, the

Fox River flowing, and the sweet butter dripping on blackened ears.

And finally, when Jill experimented with hybrid corn, she would come in with a bushel of perfect ears while I kept the kettle boiling and our children stood around with open mouths. Don once ate twelve ears, but the girls settled for six apiece. In those days, we felt corn was inedible unless it took only five minutes from garden to kettle. Since Jill's death, I have had to use store-bought corn. If you add milk, a little sugar, and seasoned salt to the boiling water, even store corn is good. And I cut the kernels from the cob afterward and brown them in butter for the next meal. It helps.

The cicada sounds the insistent note of summer. Its shrill, scraping song is part of the simmering heat, the still air, the dreaming twilight. When I look for the cockers, only dirt-frosted noses are visible as they doze in the holes they've dug beneath the shrubs. Holly, I see, has just made a special excavation under the ilex. I tell the dogs the whole yard is shady, so why do they dig? They tell me they like to lie in the moist earth. It's too warm to continue the discussion with them, and I go and get another glass of iced tea.

Jill never minded the heat; on the hottest day she'd be out working in the garden, in the full sun. By mid-August she'd be Indian-copper. Visiting small fry also pay little attention to the heat. They paddle in the pond, roll around in the sweet-smelling grass, and if they occasionally get stung by an errant bee, at least they never come home with scraped elbows or bleeding knees from falling on cement sidewalks. (I hope we never get sidewalks in our village!)

During the usual dry spell we keep an ear out for the fire siren. Fire is a threat any time of year, but especially now. A recent one began at the dump and spread rapidly. The volunteer fire department works miracles, and they checked it not far from Steve's house down the road and not very far from my meadow. Afterward we sat around the table at Steve's while Olive gave us lunch. We talked of what we would do if our houses caught fire. I knew what I would do—I would panic. I would gather the dogs and run. Olive, I felt, would get the valuables out of the house one way or another while Steve lugged water from the brook to slosh on the house.

As a nation, we seem to be incredibly careless about fire. I often see people toss cigarettes into wastebaskets or out of car windows. Sometimes when we picnic, smoldering embers mark the previous picnic someone else had. In our village, fire permits (pronounced perMITS) are needed for burning leaves and trash, but occasionally a newcomer to the valley will just "burn off" a bit of land and burn up his barn at the same time.

This is also a bad time for hay fever and asthma sufferers in our part of the country. We used to blame goldenrod for it, until somebody found out goldenrod was quite innocent. Ragweed is a menace. Jill never needed a pollen count; she had a built-in one. Nevertheless, she spent hours in the garden, only coming in when she was about to collapse and going back out the minute she could breathe again. During dry, windy spells, she said she breathed like a slow freight coming uphill. Eventually we found out that Cape Cod provided great relief. So we tried to time our visits to the Cape with the heavy pollen period at home. There is pollen on the Cape too, but apparently the kind which affected Jill most is not Cape pollen. And if the wind blows straight across the ocean from Spain, the air is completely healing.

The vastness and glory of the sea is healing too. It is there, rolling in as it has rolled since time began. Man crosses it, flies over it, goes beneath it, but the sea herself is subject to her own laws. And there are no four-lane highways on the deep. As we proceed quite systematically to ravish the land, I hope the ocean defeats us forever.

For long, hot afternoons, my friend Elizabeth Salter has her special Mint Tea, and this is her recipe. Place 1 large handful of fresh brook mint in a 2-quart container and bruise lightly. Add 4 heaping teaspoons of loose black tea on top of the mint. Pour over 4½ cups of boiling water (measure it cold and bring to boil), cover and steep 5 minutes, and then strain. It makes about 1 quart of concentrate, which will keep in the refrigerator until used. When you need it, use a 2½-quart pitcher and put in 1½ cups of sugar, 1 cup of tea concentrate, and the juice and rinds of 2 lemons and 1 orange. Fill the pitcher with ice water and some ice cubes if concentrate was used hot. You may use less sugar or more, according to taste.

Elizabeth says they drink it by the gallon, and someone once asked her if they also filled the tractor radiators with it!

My English friends say tea must always be boiling hot in hot weather. It really has a cooling effect then. But I like mine frosty cold on a hot day. Except for breakfast. Often in summer I have tea for breakfast, which is odd for a true coffee drinker. I like Earl Grey, which is supposed to be a brisk tea. I hate to admit it, but I find my tea doesn't step off in double time with a flourish of drums. It sends a good fragrance from the pot and is comfortable to drink. Of course I do not use teabags. The only tea is loose tea. I don't care for the flavor of string or thread or cheesecloth or paper or whatever else makes a bag. I want pure tea, brewed in a clean pot and served in a clean warm cup.

Most of my special hours have to do with friendship, I find. When Faith Baldwin comes, we often drive around following back roads with Holly sniffing gustily out the back window. I wish I knew the wonderful world of smell as she does. If we stop to eat, we choose a place where we can watch Holly, and this does limit the choice. I suppose there aren't too many people who would lure an Irish setter from her own car and steal her, but how do I know?

Recently on a late Sunday afternoon Steve and Olive asked me to join them for a drive. We headed toward the Berkshires, with no particular destination; we just took any road that looked inviting. We passed dreaming villages, tranquil farms, deep woods. We found a stand of white birches such as we did not know existed. We came to violet hills, folding into the deeper sky. When we stopped by a trout stream, Olive produced red caviar and onion sandwiches, thin-sliced ham and Swiss cheese, and frosty glasses of iced drinks. We drove home through a shadowy world, in which, as Olive said, nobody was about at all. We said little, just absorbing that wonderful quiet. Memory of those hours of companionship will warm me next winter when the wind roars and the snow piles up. I try to collect happy times and can highly recommend such a collection. It is far better than collecting troubled hours.

My young friend Tommy has also given me many happy memories. One of the most precious moments was the time he arrived at my door with a birthday cake, which he had baked for me himself. It was a beautiful cake! While it lasted, he came over every afternoon and we lit the candles and ate two more pieces.

When Hal and Barbara Borland come to visit, we sit around and have wonderful conversations. Sometimes we talk about Hal's latest book, or Barbara's, or mine. I've always felt that two new books by the Borlands, one by Hal and one by Barbara, provide a double treat. Her novel, *The Greater Hunger*, is a beautiful and moving story. Hal's books on nature are among the best ever written; I take a copy of *This Hill, This Valley* with me wherever I go, and I think *Sundial of the Seasons* should be on every bedside table. I have quite a Borland shelf in my library and hope to add many more books to it.

AUGUST

Some memories of friendship we especially cherish because that friend is no longer with us. Dr. Ghiselin was more than a doctor to Jill and me; he was our very good and dear friend from the day his shingle went up in our village. When this beloved physician died suddenly, everyone felt great sorrow, for this was a truly great man who actually gave his life in the service of the community. I think the loss of a good physician is hard to accept for many reasons. One feels humanity itself is the loser, for the endless years of work that go into the making of a doctor cannot be bequeathed to some new medical student. This is a road every man travels alone if he needs must take it.

The spirit of friendship contained in the many letters I receive has filled many hours over the years. Now, in August, I wait until evening to answer my mail, for the house has cooled off and I can write without mopping my face every other minute. I try to answer all the letters, except those that do not have the sender's address. I cannot keep a file of addresses—at least not if I want to LIVE in the house too, for a 1690 house was not built for filing anything! The trouble is, I cannot remember addresses. (My own family puts their house, or apartment, and street numbers on every letter!) Sometimes the name of the city or town on the postmark is clear, and I take a chance on it and always get the letter right back. Occasionally the address is there, all right, but I cannot decipher it. When I try tracing the address, which feels like a kind of forgery, this usually doesn't work either.

Occasionally I receive letters addressed to *Gladys Taber, Writer, Connecticut,* and am always amazed at the postal department. One Sunday the postmaster from the nearest big city came with his wife to call because, he said, he wanted to meet the woman who got all that poorly addressed mail!

A good part of my mail is forwarded from the *Family Circle* office, and sometimes the outer envelope is missing. It should be fairly easy to put one's address at the top of the page beginning *Dear Mrs. Taber* plus the date, so I can figure out how long the letter has been in the office. But many people will make the effort to write an interesting letter and then make it impossible for me to answer. I always feel sure they think I am an unkind, selfish person to ignore them.

If postal rates keep jumping, the time will come when it is cheaper to send day telegrams! I found some dear old one-cent postcards when I was cleaning out my desk not long ago and eyed them wistfully. There were also some two-cent stamped envelopes. Oh, the lovely bygone days!

One day this summer Joe arrived with his wonderful electric saw and sawed up a pile of fallen timber and stacked it. The pile reached to the window sill, and so it looks as if I have firewood for several years. Faith Baldwin was here and commented that the sound of an electric saw is definitely mean. Vicious and snarling. It is not a sound to be ignored.

When the job was finished, Joe came in for coffee. Erma joined us, and we sat and talked about the diseases of trees and how to graft wildlings and what is the best bird cover. I don't know when I've enjoyed anything so much. It is rewarding, in this explosive age, to visit with people who wish to preserve nature's gifts and cherish them.

As time goes on, it will be harder to keep what we still have. I am sad when I think that sooner or later our village will no longer be the small, intimate place it has been, summer and winter, since the Revolution. Already a new throughway has sliced through the edge of the hills and woods. Big machines have chewed away at the loveliest stand of woods, the gentlest slope, the beautiful meadow once starred with bluets. I wonder why progress wears such an ugly face.

Of course, I am grateful that my own forty acres did not lie in the path of the highway; nor did Steve and Olive's property, though that was a near miss. But my heart goes out to those who will wake in the morning to the sound of rushing traffic instead of bird song. It is hard not to grieve over what is being done to the beauty of America.

My pond grows low in August and we begin to worry about the water table. It occurs to me there is not enough water anywhere any more, and if we continue to denude the land we may well have gigantic dust bowls all over the country. In our village, sparked by George Bennet's patient and untiring work, we work at conservation. Literally thousands of pines, cedars, autumn olives, and nut trees have been planted. We have a program for flood control (2,000 willow cuttings last spring for erosion control along the streams).

A couple of years ago, George and a group of Boy Scouts planted pines on a steep, eroding slope above my beloved swamp. Now it is a wildlife haven and winter shelter for the birds (who keep the insect invasion down) and a bulwark against drifting snows. The swamp was drying out; now I note water stands in it again. And my surface well held up all last summer.

I love my well. It is protected by the well house, where wisteria blooms in season. You can lift the lid and look down into the cool, dark depths and smell the sweet, icy water. You can also drop a dogfood can in it, as Don did; or let your glasses fall down, as Ed Koch once did. Retrieving such things involves a slippery, hazardous descent from wet stone to wetter stone and fishing around with a rake. Whoever is brave enough to do this cleans the well—and emerges dripping with a pailful of oddments. Then we empty the water tank and start again.

Much as we loved the old ways, Jill decided when we bought Stillmeadow that hauling water up with a crank was just *too* much, so a modern electric pump brings it to the tank in the cellar. It isn't romantic, but it is easy!

Last spring, I took another drastic step away from the olden days. I put in an exhaust fan over the range. It meant cutting a hole outside in the ancient hand-cut clapboards I love dearly, but the children had come every week end and it seemed to me we were always cooking pork chops and cabbage and bacon and Vienna sausage. And the day we all went off to the ski run leaving the big copper spider on the stove with ¼ inch of sausage fat in it and the heat under it was an argument that convinced me. The house was so full of greasy smoke you could slice it and spread it on bread if you wanted to. The hole outside isn't very noticeable, and the Irish and the cockers enjoy it immensely.

They can bed down in the violet bed and doze until they smell what's cooking. Then it's time to get up and come in!

For years I used to think there would come a day when everything worked, everything was in repair at *one time*.

I once defined maturity as the art of being willing to shell peas, but now I think it is accepting cheerfully the fact that something is always out of order. Once I felt heady with triumph as I had my breakfast on the terrace. Even the toaster was fixed. A state of euphoria is what I was in. That night I called Willie, my neighbor around the corner, and said the furnace had gone off with a series of explosions. Willie spent some time communing with the burner in the cellar and then fixed it. Afterward he explained all about the valve to me. So now I have decided there is no such thing as a home all fixed and everything in working order at one time.

At night I like to take a cup of coffee to the terrace and watch the dogs chase imaginary things. Only an occasional diminished *whirro* accents the quiet. I cannot see my neighbors' lights through the heavy foliage, but I can see the moonlight making patterns on the pond.

The full sturgeon moon burns slowly across the hazy sky; shadows lengthen. Holly appears, carrying a pink woolly rabbit she appropriated last time the family were here. I wonder which one is howling because the pet "wabbit" is missing! Children, I reflect, always seem to leave their favorite toys behind—the ones necessary for survival.

The month is almost at an end. Summer—summer—it ends too soon, too soon. But when I ask the cockers and Holly if they mind another winter coming, they say they can't be bothered about it. They live in the moment, as we

AUGUST

all should do more often. They savor the rich, heavy air of August and find things to chase by the woodpile. Tomorrow will be as it may be, they feel. They are right: I think most of us spend too much time living in the past or trying to live in the future. Meanwhile, today is all we have. And today has infinite possibilities. It is ours to make what we will of it.

September

ONE MORNING I go out to pick wild asters and suddenly it is September at Stillmeadow. I think it is the smell of the air, like wild grapes and windfall apples. I know fall is here, although the world is still green with summer. And I feel an urgency to gather in all the loveliness of the past blazing days and star-cool nights and keep them forever.

The Stillmeadow road is edged now with gold. From the picket fence I look up the hill to the mailbox and see the wave of goldenrod, accented with the purple of wild asters. It gives me a sense of sadness, lovely as it is, for goldenrod is the forerunner of the bright, cool autumn which will make our valley blaze with glory. Hal Borland tells me he once counted 3,023 individual flowers on a spray of goldenrod. I don't know whether I was more impressed by the number or by Hal's matchless patience. I would have been in a state of collapse by the time I got up to 45. And when Hal went on to say that with a magnifying glass he studied the individual florets and found there were 20,000 in an average plume, it seemed unbelievable. What invention of man could be more intricate than a spray of this country weed?

Days grow shorter now and migrant birds leave according to their own mysterious schedule. Squirrels fling themselves from tree to tree in a burst of activity. I always hope they store enough hickory nuts and acorns, but they never do. What they do is eat the bird food from the feeders and clean up everything put out for the chickadees, nuthatches, woodpeckers, and juncoes. The woodchucks are busy too. Now and then an overstuffed one gets in the road and is run down—but not by me. And there is no shooting done on my acres except when the children bang away at a tomato can nailed to a post. So the wild people can go about their business as I go about mine.

Now that so much of the woodlands has been destroyed, I sometimes wonder just how many dwellers there are in my woods and swamps. Most of the deer have gone and this is a sad loss. We used to stop the car on Jeremy Swamp Road while two or three deer crossed over. The movement of a deer is like a madrigal, and a wobbly fawn adds a grace note. I have always wanted my own personal deer, not to pen up but just to know. But then I have also always wanted a seal. Probably the reason the swamp is what I love best in my forty acres is that it is a haven for all kinds of wildlife, from ruffed grouse to cardinals. The bushes and plants stand with their feet in water, and somehow a brook runs into one end and vanishes. Cranberries grow at one edge and they are big as birds' eggs, pale gold in color tinged with red, and sweet as honey. You have to crawl to reach them, being very careful not to get too far in the bog. I fell in once and was dragged out by Jill with difficulty. But we knew we had no right to invade the swamp in the first place. It belongs to itself, not to man, and it goes about its important business of preserving what we call the balance of nature.

At the end of the swamp, a narrow road turns right to the house. The giant sugar maples that surround it are spreading a deep green canopy above the slant roof and I look up at them and tell them that the first swamp maple is turning. Whether they believe me or not, I do not know. They are inscrutable. They are also very independent. Sometimes the biggest one at the corner of the yard will be summer green while the one back where the barn burned is flaming with glory. Why?

Weather conditions are the same for all of them, one is no more sheltered than another, and they are the same age, judging by their size. I like to think one tree decides to keep summer a bit longer and one impetuously responds to the tide of oncoming autumn. Trees are not remotely like people, but I reflect that I know some people who have never let summer go and others who begin to think winter thoughts in July. Perhaps it is all temperament.

After summer's work is over, there is an interval before autumn chores begin. What better time to follow some winding country road? One day Erma and I explored the

Palestine district. The meadows are marked by gray stone fences in better condition than any others I have seen. Clear brooks run beside the road and small ponds reflect the blue sky. Old farmhouses dream in the slanting shadows of sugar maples. Erma said we hadn't accomplished much that day but we could think of those pleasant hours, come January.

My California son-in-law Curt says he will never get used to the narrow, wandering roads of New England. It is true they take their time getting anywhere, and many of them are too narrow for two cars to pass unless one squeezes off the road. Some of them were Indian trails and some led from one homestead to another. The Stillmeadow road was the old Kettletown road which fell into disuse for a long time. Kettletown was bought from the Indians for a copper kettle, and a settlement was begun there. Now all that is left is an old cemetery with the graves of a few Revolutionary soldiers. I've always wondered what happened. We used to picnic there at the edge of the deep woods, and we felt the strangeness in the air.

When the leaves begin to turn, it seems everyone wants to see the splendor. I notice that people, wherever they are, want to go somewhere else. Travelers come from everywhere to our hills, while some of us go to the Berkshires. On Cape Cod, people go to Vermont for "fall coloring." New Yorkers and Midwesterners go to Cape Cod to see the garnet cranberry bogs and blue-gray bayberries. It doesn't matter, really. The desire to look at beauty is the important thing.

Later this month, two major events will occur—the line storm and the black frost. The line storm can be like a hurricane with terrible rain and heavy winds, and I have to stuff bath towels around the windows and doorsills. The frost comes after a still day, and we do not need weather reports to know it is coming. We feel it. The day after it comes, the vegetable garden looks as if it had been ironed. Flowers hang limp on blackened stalks. There will be more balmy weather, of course, and Jill used to say if she could just wrap that frost up and put it down cellar, there would be more tomatoes, more corn, more everything. And I used to say I had had enough of canning, preserving, pickling, and freezing and the sight of one more jelly bag dripping in the kitchen would drive me out of my mind!

Now school begins again and I listen for the school bus to swing along Jeremy Swamp Road. It carries my young neighbor Tommy, who pops in and out daily, but now he can only come after the bus drops him off, and how eagerly I await his visit. He gives me a report on what has gone on in a world I cannot enter. I almost envy his teacher, for Tommy has a quicksilver mind and great sensitivity.

I may be wrong, but I think country children have an early sense of responsibility that apartment children do not get. "I think I'll clean out the woodshed," says Tommy, "before the cold comes." Or, "Time to get cedar chips for the kennel." Or, "I'm going to see if I can hammer the gate latch back."

He fixes a great many things for me. And his latest project was rebuilding a discarded sewing-machine motor.

"Of course you can't do anything with it," he said modestly, "but it runs!"

"Well," I said, "the most important thing is that it runs."

After all, I reflected, much in life seems to have no tangible result, just as many roads we follow seem to have no ending. But it isn't necessary always to have a useful practical result. It's the going ahead that matters.

Sometimes I come back from the village behind the school bus. I like to see the children tumble out, two at one house, three at another, one at a third. Free temporarily, the small boys jump up and down and throw things and the girls tend to ignore them and walk sedately to the house. It makes me think every house should always have a couple of small children coming home from school. But you cannot always keep children on hand; they have a way of growing up.

School is very important nowadays. I cannot get used to the fact that a child can never miss a day at nursery school unless he has measles or mumps or a virus. Then there is kindergarten from which the child graduates! I never attended either, which is one reason I could always go off with Father when he hunted for specimens. I never even learned to make paper chains, but I was a very good finder of Indian arrows. Father taught me a lot of incidental things, such as how to tell which way the glacier moved and what to do if lost in the woods (I never was) and what a drumline was.

Father raised me to believe leisure was almost a sin. You had to be actively doing something every waking minute, and I still feel a little guilty when I just do nothing but sit and think long thoughts. Mama had a reflective temperament, but in our household life was an express train. The only quiet times Mama and I had were when Father was teaching a class at college with a lab session. Then we would have afternoon tea and feel peaceful. I have noticed since that dynamic people are uncomfortable unless everyone around is being dynamic too!

I am always being told by the rest of the family and my relatives that I am just like my father. But I think this is only a top layer of resemblance, for I like quietude as Mama did.

I have found that when I cannot possibly accomplish everything I am supposed to, and I feel an unbearable pressure, as all homemakers must, if I just STOP, life goes better. I get a good book, like Hal Borland's *Countryman*, and make some Constant Comment tea, and sit down on my own corner of the sofa or in my favorite lawn chair. I let life settle in around me—and that's the only way I can express it. After twenty minutes or half an hour, I go back to the mechanics of living. And at day's end, I am just as far along as if I hadn't stopped to think!

I wish I could share this recipe with the children, who seem to be trying to compress a lifetime of work into every twenty-four hours. But time for thinking is a gift you can only give yourself. The whole pace of today's civilization is against it. "I just don't have time to read," a good many people say to me. But when I consider that all history, all of men's dreams, all hopes are there to share in books, I wonder what is so important that there is no time to read. Or, "I have no time to listen to music," says a harried friend. And yet music, which enlarges the mind and lifts the soul, is so available. I was reminded of this recently when I turned my radio on for the latest dire news and got all of *Tosca*, with Robert Merrill singing. I threw my list of absolutely vital chores in the fire and listened to *Tosca*.

With the arrival of this comfortable season, pleasantly balmy at noon and refreshingly cool at twilight, I inevitably consider airing things, and Erma discusses fall cleaning with me as we sit at the counter drinking coffee. My tendency is to throw all the tea-colored ruffled curtains in the dump. Not at all, says Erma firmly. She will do them by hand and they will last another season. I mention painting the white woodwork, now grimy and black with prints of small hands. Not at all, she decides, she will wash it and it will go another round. I tell her the washing machine isn't working, and she gets down on her knees and opens it up and communes with it and extracts a dry quart of diaper lint. It then works. No use spending money, she says. I wouldn't want to add up the money Erma has saved me, but I suppose it would almost pay for a trip to London.

In my childhood, almost everything movable went out of the house spring and fall. Mama would use the vacuum all year long, but in May and September the rugs were still put out and beaten with a fancy wire whip. Curtains, drapes, bedding—these went too, as did the upholstered pieces. Freshens them up, she said. So my passion for airing may be a heritage.

In the early days at Stillmeadow, Jill and I even got the mattresses out, and when they were laid in the sun a bevy of cocker puppies bounced on them with cries of joy. It was rather like trampolin practice. We hung the rugs on the picket fence and every puppy tugged at the fringes.

"I'm not sure we are really accomplishing much," Jill said.

I've given up on mattresses and the nine-by-twelve braided rug. But everything easy to carry goes out and gets freshened up in the old-fashioned way. Erma, who helps with this project, agrees with me. The dryer is fine in winter, when sheets freeze before you can put on the clothespins outdoors, but now the wash is hung out in the golden air. We do not iron the sheets either; we let the smell of sun stay with them, along with the whiff of pine.

It is always nice to have a new book come out, with its record of many feelings, much thought, and some dreaming. It doesn't seem to have anything to do with all the hours of work. I admire the jacket, and feel the smooth paper, and feel pleased that my gentle publisher has done such a lovely job. An hour later I begin to think: it's time to start work on a new one and not just sit idly in the sun. As my father used to say, "If you don't get started, you never get anywhere."

Most of us spend a lot of time seeking happiness and

always feel we shall achieve it magically. We translate our yearning into symbols—a new house, a bigger and better car, a place in the country or a place in the city, a collection of something special, or a rare painting worth more money than we have. We want material success for our children along with ease of living and more luxuries than we had when we were their age. And then most of us wonder that happiness doesn't come to sit by our fireside. If we are fortunate, we realize at some point in our search that we are taking the wrong path. Happiness is, in the end, an attitude of mind. It involves acceptance of reality and a warm appreciation of such simple things as a friend looking happy when we meet unexpectedly or the way the first star comes out at twilight. It means an open heart.

We can never be insulated against disaster or suffering or grief, for these inevitably come to all of us. Nevertheless, as long as we are a part of time for our brief moment, we can be happy because the moon rises in her accustomed way, a song sparrow sings to establish the boundaries of his own area, the earth turns in her own orbit. We now know there are many solar systems besides ours and the earth may be an inconsequential planet, but it is our own.

Some people believe that man's destructive instincts will fade in time and the world will become less addicted to wars and conflict and hate. I for one think this is likely, for I have faith in mankind. Most of my lifetime has been spent in the shadow of war, and yet, in this same period, social consciousness has awakened. The rich and privileged and secure now care about the poor and troubled and deprived. We pass laws to help them, and laws are nothing but a reflection of man's thinking. My father believed that if you were *good* and worked hard, all things would come to you. I'm afraid if he heard of any long-overdue poverty program he would simply say, "What's wrong with those people? Why don't they get out and work?"

But times have really changed so that most of us now realize that socio-economic conditions affect people whether people are good or not. We have no choice as to when or where we are born or what color we are.

A few men can rise above any sort of deprived backgrounds, but what about the others? They need education, a reasonable diet, and a chance to develop their own assets. Plants grow spindly and weak in poor soil and bear no fruit; given proper care, they would grow tall and firm and give abundantly. Surely every child born today should have as much care as a stand of corn.

But, said a friend of mine, there are a lot of retarded and disturbed people in the world. You are not going to make senators of them.

Yes, this is true. But one of the most rewarding jobs we are beginning to do is the work on mental retardation, its underlying causes, and what can be done about it. We can no longer shrug our shoulders and say, "Well, of course, he is one of those." For we have a responsibility to him too.

The rise of juvenile delinquency is alarming. My friend Hal Borland wrote me that one night all the mailboxes on their country road were run into, knocked down, and if possible run over and smashed. This kind of senseless vandalism is fairly prevalent. But I have to balance it against 500 students graduating from a big regional high school where my friends Helen and Vicky teach. Many of them are going on to higher education and will form a basis for a good society. They are alert, thinking young people, avid for knowledge. They reach out, says Helen, for all you can give them.

I am not a trained social worker or a psychiatrist; I am just a parent. But I feel a deep sorrow for these troubled youngsters who have to "get even with the world." Somewhere someone has not given them anything to aim at. So all they can do is smash mailboxes, wreck Southern towns on vacation, run their cars head-on into collisions. Why do they not channel their energy, which is boundless, into something constructive? Why are they the lost, the doomed? I noted during devastating floods one winter that the teen-agers were the most valiant volunteers of all, working on the dikes, lugging the sandbags. And a good many college students have spent their spring vacations in the South helping rebuild bombed Negro churches.

I cannot help feeling that the teen-agers who jam the Southern beaches for "sun, suds, sand, and sex" just don't know what to do with themselves. So their energy explodes. I am sorry for them, and sorry for their parents and their schools. I don't believe it is all the fault of parents and schools, however. Parents have been blamed for everything for some time now; it is the fashion. Inefficient schools are partly a cause, but certainly not major. I am not wise enough certainly to offer a solution, except that I find the teen-agers I know who are most stable, most responsive, better behaved are those who have learned the discipline of work very early. Boys and girls who take jobs during vacations seem to get into less trouble. Those with fast cars, plenty of money, and nothing definite to do tend to make trouble.

One sad effect of this is that adults begin to look suspiciously at every teen-ager. "Better watch out, he's sixteen," I often hear, or, "I wouldn't let him come around too much —you know those teen-agers." And even the steadiest hardworking teen-agers often find it difficult to get jobs that involve responsibility.

"But you know Jim is one of the nicest boys——"

"Yes, but you don't know who his friends are! Don't have him mow the lawn unless you are at home. No telling what might happen."

I do not think this is a very constructive attitude. It would never suit me, for I trust everyone except those few men and women who seem to enjoy spreading rumors about people. Perhaps I trust everyone because of reacting against my father, who was suspicious of almost anyone. Whenever anything was missing, he at once decided the cleaning woman had taken it. When it turned up in whatever place he had tucked it away, he never stopped to wonder. If he mislaid a tool, he always felt a neighbor had lifted it. He was sure the tax money was lining some-body's pockets.

He suspected Mama of giving some of the housekeeping money to needy passers-by (good-for-nothing tramps). He suspected me of not telling him everything. Both Mama and I felt the less he knew about some things the more peaceful life was! Father was an exuberant, fascinating man with an exceedingly brilliant scientific mind. He had many talents; for example, he played the violin well enough to pay his way through college doing so. He was a top hockey player, a crack shot, an engaging conversationalist. He was, inci-dentally, handsome. However, his complete lack of faith in human beings was a severe handicap and, I think, shad-owed his life.

I would rather be taken advantage of now and then than go around suspecting every stranger of wanting to take ad-vantage of me. And I have wondered whether my faith in people might be one reason why it has so seldom happened to me. Or perhaps I am blessed in having known so many honest folk! In any case, it makes for a happier life for me, and when a friend says ominously, "I wouldn't trust that one around the corner!" I usually say, "Why not? Might as well."

Pursuing this thought in a larger area, I think the trouble between nations is quite simple. No nation fails to suspect all other nations, and no nation ever really trusts another. As I write, every nation in the world seems to be sure my own country is steeped with ambition to rule every country in the world, not to mention space. I hear we have a bad image abroad. I hear it, in fact, incessantly. Apparently America is more prosperous than most and this is a dire omen. We also have a good army and navy and a stable government. Therefore we are imperialists and must somehow be defeated. We pour millions into many countries in aid, but when did a poor relation ever really love and admire the rich one who donated the gifts? It is hard to be a happy receiver of largesse, and I expect this is a basic trait in human nature. It implies a failure on the part of the recipient and suggests a condescension.

I once had a friend who came to me in tears.

"You know ——— is desperately poor," she said, "and I would so love to help her. But, Gladys, I can't even give her an apron without her getting furious! I made her such a pretty one, and she said she didn't need an apron."

It may be more blessed to give than to receive, but it is also blessed to receive graciously.

September meals are no problem, except how to keep up with the vegetables. I eat tomatoes at least twice a day. The season is all too short for sun-ripened tomatoes. I like them fried for breakfast. I first fry thin slices of bacon until very crisp. Then I take the bacon from the pan and cut tomatoes in half, dip them in seasoned flour, and fry them in the bacon drippings, turning only once. I garnish them with chopped parsley.

If I am having company for supper, I do my Fried Tomato Bake because I can get it ready ahead of time. I dredge tomato halves in flour or cornmeal, add salt and pepper, and fry them in drippings or butter, turning once. Allow 2 small (or 1 medium) per person. Arrange the pieces in a deep buttered casserole, top with buttered crumbs, and bake in a hot oven (400°) for 20 minutes before suppertime. I've even fixed this dish the night before. (And how I appreciate the new casserole ware that goes directly from refrigerator to oven without any danger of breaking!)

Recipes are never-ending with me. When I wrote *Stillmeadow Cook Book,* I felt I had enough recipes to last the rest of my life. I would simply go on using them because there were plenty. But I am a hopeless addict. I read cookbooks; I read all the recipes in the magazines, including every single one in the ads. I clip and clip and clip. I copy friends' recipes. I dream up new ones. And only the other day, as I cleaned the herb shelf, I found myself thinking dreamily, "I might just do a week-end cookbook some day . . ."

September and October are both good months to be on Cape Cod. When I come from the inland wooded hills and deeply shaded valleys and see the Cape, lying low and open to the sky, it seems to be the home of light itself. The pines are low and wind-bent and the undergrowth is low too, trimmed by nor'easters. The houses are fitted in as if they grew behind the low picket fences. White is the typical house color in my valley, and gray is the color of the Cape houses. The shingles are left to weather, and salt and blown sand silver them. The Cape roads wander past salt marshes, bogs, bayberry thickets, and sweet-water ponds. But they invariably end at either the ocean or bayside.

The summer visitors leave around Labor Day, usually going back to jobs and school. Cottages are boarded up, boats lifted from the water, beaches are wide and quiet, and it is rather like the curtain going down on Act III. Then villages lie in tranquil sunlight and people walk slowly to the post offices, no longer dodging cars. The opinion of the Cape Cod residents is, "I am sorry they have to go, poor things, but I'm glad they're gone."

Most of what has been written about Cape Codders is not true. They are not quaint characters; they are sturdy, independent, and wise folk. Perhaps living within sound of the sea has given them a better perspective on life. Most of the Cape people I have grown to love have a sense of humor that is quick but rarely unkind. They are unusually friendly and generous—this may be a legacy from the days when their lives depended on their all working together, with and against the great sea. I have never asked a Cape Codder for help in vain—and no thanks expected, either.

True, I did want to buy a pink lawn chair once from a Cape dealer who had some fifty chairs of assorted colors; but he would not sell me the pink one. It was his, he said. The month being October, his chance of selling the other forty-nine chairs diminished hourly. But the pink one was not for sale. I agree with him that if a thing is yours you needn't sell it!

Since the Cape no longer depends on fishing for support —although there are still a number who gather the sea's rich crops for a living—and cranberry picking is seasonal, the economy of the Cape is built chiefly around the summer people. They buy land at high prices, build houses, shop with intensity, and will pay anything to get a small load of firewood. The main trouble with them is they all get vacations in July and August, and there is really not enough room on the narrow land for them all at once. That is why the year-rounders begin to lead normal lives only when September comes.

A good many of them have relatives and guests all summer long. They do not expect to see their Cape friends until after Labor Day, and then casual suppers, afternoon parties, and coffee-and-desserts begin. It is as if they had all been on a long journey and had at last reached home port. I visit Charlotte and Ruth in their exquisite house with the whole sea spread before it and sweet gardens frilled around it like ladies' Victorian laces. I take a Sunday afternoon ride with Bobby Gibson and see roads I never saw before. (Sunday afternoon rides were the high point in my childhood, and I wish they would come back.) I watch football with Millie and Ed after a superb dinner. I sit by the fire at Helen's and talk books. Or worry over a crossword that seems impossible to do with Margaret while we eat her famous baked beans. These are just a few of the happy meetings that belong to September when life is so tender!

And I wish it could go on forever. I do not even mind paying a dollar and a half for fourteen small, undernourished pieces of firewood, although at Stillmeadow my woodpile reaches to the window sills outside two rooms and the wood is prime.

One Sunday on the Cape stands out in my memory. My cousin Rob and his wife Bebe were coming for breakfast. I decided to go along with the experts who advise a hearty one. I set the time at twelve, figuring I could be waked up by then. I splurged on Rock Cornish game hens on the theory they were lighter than chicken. I made a ·pilaf because something had to go with the birds, and since I had a can of beets I fixed Harvard beets to give a color contrast.

Rob had gone out at six, however, and found a clam bed, so my guests arrived with a huge pail of clams. We began with a platter of cherrystones (accompanied by horse-radish, lemon, catsup). We then consumed half a gallon of steamers with a pint of broth to each. Then came my part of the meal. And as he finished his Cornish hen Rob suddenly said, "You forgot the salad!"

It is now referred to as that breakfast with no salad.

My favorite in the clam family is the small quahog. These are known as cherrystones in the city and as "the little ones" on the Cape. You need a clam rake, a wire basket, and determination—that's all. Somehow the clamming itself is sheer joy, for the water is still and lovely and the only sound is the lonely cry of gulls riding the air currents. Sometimes, as you stop to rest, you see a freighter far out, bound for a distant land.

The clams are cool to the touch and almost iridescent. I have never learned how to open them, but Rob says it is because I make them nervous. He evidently calms them, for we have a platterful in no time. Rob likes a sauce of hot horse-radish, lemon, and catsup, but there's a lot to be said for plain lemon juice and pepper. The Cape clams are delicate pink and honey-sweet, and all you need for a meal is fresh Portuguese bread with garlic butter. And plenty of hot coffee.

There is color on the Cape in October, but not the flaming passionate colors you find inland. There is some low oak with brown-red leaves, there are thickets that turn rosy brown, and there is the lovely gray-blue of the bayberries. And of course the cranberry bogs, which spread like a jeweled carpet. And finally, there is the ocean, which is every color there is according to weather and light. Is it more beautiful as the sky turns apricot and the sea is washed with pink as the sun sinks—or when the great blue-green seas reaching out toward Spain deepen to indigo at twilight? Is it more beautiful when the tide is out and the clam flats are polished pewter, with pools of pink pearl here and there—or when the white crests roll in at full tide, flinging salt spray on the great beach? And at night, when the moon floats on the deep sea of sky and casts a shining path over black deep water—perhaps this is loveliest? I am glad I do not have to choose. I can have them all.

All summer Holly and the cockers pursued a snake that lives in the terrace. Holly has a particular snake bark, and there is fear in it. For some reason the snake always got away.

Now, before hundreds of people write me that snakes are wonderful, I will agree. I never went on any snake hunts, never killed any that were not directly underfoot and frightening Jill. And she let spiders (which frighten me) alone except when they invaded the house. But I don't think even a snake fan would like to descend the steep cellar stairs and step right on a five-foot black snake. Or find one curled up in the kennel near a bevy of eight-week-old cockers.

We had, once, one golden cocker named, incorrectly, Silver Moon (she was white when born). Moon killed snakes. We must have had a couple of hundred dogs when we were raising them, but only Moon would come to the house proudly bearing a snake.

They were hard to carry, and Moon would have to stop now and then to adjust her grip. I always knew what was up, because Jill, the quietest person I ever knew, would utter a sound like a fire siren as Moon approached with the present.

It is interesting to speculate on mankind's common fear of snakes. I've been told it is because primitive man feared the snakes that dropped on him from trees. But why do my dogs have the same aversion? Holly could catch that snake in a minute if she had her heart in it.

September is a good time for the Irish and the cockers. Raccoons are about, eating the best of the corn, woodchucks come right in the back yard at times, and the squirrels are there for chasing. The dogs like to stay out late hunting things they almost never catch. What they *do* catch is nettles and sticktights and burs, but that is part of the game. Teddy is the gentlest golden boy but last week, when a possum came in the run, something just came over him and he killed it. He had, he said, protected me from an invader. I should just put my mind at ease, he would take care of things. I felt sad, for I love all wild woods folk, but I decided a sign saying POSSUMS GO AWAY wouldn't help.

The other day Holly took a notion to bring in some fallen branches, one by one. Trying to fetch just half a branch through a regular-size door kept her busy for quite a while, but she figured out that by going sideways she could get through. She laid the branches on my bed, scattering twigs of course, all over the floor. Then she lay down on the bed next to them and slept with her paws folded tenderly over the branches.

September is a special grace for those of us who face a long, bitter New England winter. Summer's lease has been all too short; now it is over. Nature is at her mysterious work of turning leaves, putting gardens to bed, signaling the wildlife to prepare for the heavy snows. Those that hibernate are fortunate, it seems to me, for they just move into their burrows for a long dream. Those that do not must, like summer birds, migrate or eke out a hard existence in the zero temperatures. Since I cannot hibernate or migrate, I lay aside a store of emergency foods, hunt up my boots and storm clothes, and ask the furnace man to clean the oil burner and check the fireplace flue.

How good it is to come into the house at teatime and enjoy the heartwarming sight of the hearth fire again! I sit beside it and reflect that I may as well throw away that list of "Things to Do This Summer." I made it in April, and not a great deal of it can be crossed off now. But there's always time to make another one on a snowbound winter day!

The harvest moon is heavy with gold; the stars are polished diamonds. The dogs and I walk out onto the lawn; a fox barks in the woods, otherwise the night is wondrously still. Beautiful pale smoke floats up from the ancient chimney, and I think of Thoreau's words: "There is no remedy for love but to love." That's how I feel about September, and I wish I could share the tranquility of this night with my unknown neighbors all over the world.

Sidonie Coryn

October

THE WILD GEESE went over early one morning this week. Why this is so moving, I do not know. All of us feel it; in the village store someone says, "I heard the geese go over," and there is a moment of silence. We seldom make much of the swallows or other migratory birds when they leave, although we are very likely to note the red-wings when they come back in March. But the geese—ah, that is to feel a quickening of the heart.

High and lovely, they wedge through the sky, their faint cries drifting down to earth, and for a brief time we seem to fly too. How do they chart their course? How many miles do they travel? How many of them fail to make it? How do they know when they've reached their destination? And how high do they fly? Perhaps higher than other birds . . .

Days grow shorter now, the nights chillier. Crisp mornings call for buttermilk pancakes and maple syrup, with country sausage on the side; at supper the popovers are almost too hot to hold. The trees kindle with color, a few at a time: small flashes of scarlet appear in the swamp, and the sugar maples begin to glow, as the great wave of autumn glory slowly rises to full tide. Leaves start to fall; I pick one up. It is cool to the touch; a hint of pink lies under the gold. As it dries, the serrated edges curl inward and the leaf turns to tawny brown. I think, I am holding autumn in my hand.

As the trees give up their summer finery, the world around me comes into view once more. I can see the postman stopping at the mailboxes along the road, the lights at suppertime glowing in kitchen windows. It is pleasant to have my horizon widened again! I always *know* Willie and Wilma are just around the bend on Jeremy Swamp Road, but it's nice to *see* neighbors' rooftops and chimneys and windows.

Where only a month ago the valley was clothed in emerald, it is now clad in mustard gold, peppery red, and nutmeg brown. The cockers jump and roll in heaps of leaves and then dash into the house, where they shed autumn drifts of color on the rug and hearth. When Teddy flings himself into a carefully raked pile of leaves, he vanishes up to his eyebrows. It takes him no time at all to demolish one hour's work!

What is better than watching a dark-red Irish setter chasing a red-red falling leaf? It is great sport, Holly tells me when she stops to catch her breath, and I often think I would like to join in the fun. Perhaps she and the cockers want to make the most of every golden October hour. The wildfolk are preparing for the long cold ahead, but my dogs take no thought for the morrow. They figure it's my responsibility anyway—a sensible point of view, after all!

When I go for a drive these days, I notice the bustle of activity in the valley. Bent figures are visible in most gardens as women go out to put in a few more spring bulbs. There is something symbolic about this fall planting, for it reflects a looking forward to spring with confidence. Most of the bulbs resemble small onions with papery skins, and the idea that beauty will emerge from them seems strange. I have a friend who once cooked up a mess of what she thought were onions when she was in a hurry. It turned out they were most expensive flower bulbs! Inedible, she said sorrowfully.

Jill taught me to stand and toss handfuls of bulbs casually on the ground and then plant them where they fell. This naturalized planting is far better than putting them in rows or circles or stars or whatever. Most bulbs come with directions as to how deep and in what kind of soil to plant them, but I simply plant them any place I think I would like them, and the Connecticut soil is favorable to them.

My favorite of all the spring bulbs is the Mt. Hood daffodil, and last year a friend sent a whole carton of them to me. My second choice is the King Alfred, and I planted both on a slope where they opened in a way that reminded me of Wordsworth's host of daffodils. I am putting in more bulbs this month, including some new varieties that are completely strange to me, and next year I shall do the same, for who could have enough of them? This past year I was very lucky, for there were too many rabbits around for comfort, and about the only thing they didn't eat were the daffodils. A nurseryman tells me he has given up on tulips. Nothing is prettier than a small bunny in the sweet clover, but rabbits rampant in the vegetable rows are not as adorable! They begin by eating the tips of the asparagus in May and chomp along on everything from then on. Olive, down the road, reports that one late afternoon she looked out of the kitchen window and saw her husband racing after a huge rabbit. They went by the window, and presently went by again, and then reversed their courses the third time around the house so the rabbit was behind Steve. She leaned out and called, "Who's chasing whom?"

Roadside stands splash more color along the roads now, and I wish I could paint them. Great smoky blue Hubbard squash, dark green acorn squash, bright orange pumpkins, strings of Chinese lanterns, baskets of rosy apples and bouquets of bittersweet, and sometimes Indian corn and gourds —all make a carnival of autumn and testify to nature's endless bounty. Jugs of freshly pressed cider stand in the cool shade, as well as jars of clover honey. Sometimes there are new-laid eggs for sale, or homemade jellies, lucent in the sun, or rich preserves and jars of crisp pickles, and sometimes loaves of fresh homemade bread and pans of crusty rolls. It is fun to stop to visit with the men who keep the stands and talk crops and gardens. And when you arrive home, the back seat is full of special things you just couldn't resist buying.

It is not too early to decorate Stillmeadow for autumn. Pumpkins go on each side of the front door, a sheaf of corn dresses up the Dutch door, and a Hubbard squash by the well house is just right. I suppose this custom goes back to the days when men propitiated the gods of the harvest by offering the yield of the summer as a sacrifice. Many of our traditions go back into the mists of time, when we stop to think of it. Lighted candles have more meaning than the electric lamps, for instance. Our devotion to an open fire surely is reminiscent of the time when man discovered the benison of a warm blaze at the cave entrance.

There are many theories about the discovery of fire—perhaps lightning struck a fallen tree and fire began there, but I think we shall never know. But we do know that before fire was discovered man ate everything raw, which I find a horrifying thought!

At long last, I have learned about gourds. Jill and I gave up raising them, for sometimes they kept but more often they disintegrated into spongy masses in the copper bowl. We tried waxing them, shellacking them, putting them in the cold woodshed to season, putting them on top of the well house. Now my friend Elsie Dawson writes that if the vines freeze *before* the gourds ripen, the gourds do not keep. If they harden and ripen on the vine before freezing, they are fine. The pulp dries by itself into nothingness, leaving only the seeds. In case you want a percussion instrument, you have it! Or you can cut the gourds in half and use them as dippers or bowls. Had we known this, we might have put mittens on the vines and enjoyed a good crop of gourds regularly.

When the children come for week ends now, I have the soup kettle simmering. One favorite is a fish chowder which my Cape Cod friend, Phil Schwind, generously shared with me last year. It is called Aunt Beulah's Fish Chowder and came down to him from his Aunt Beulah. I wish I could repeat it the way he described it, including directions as to burying the fish heads deep near the grapevine, the finest kind of fertilizer. But space requires me to condense it. You make it from haddock back, tautog, cusk, striper, or flounder, using a pound of fillets. Wash these and simmer 20 minutes in 2 cups of cold water (it doesn't stay cold, of course). Cut or break the fish into 2-inch pieces. Strain and save the fish water.

Cut a 1½-inch piece of salt pork into small cubes and fry out to golden brown in the chowder kettle. Remove the pieces and brown 1 medium-sized sliced onion in the hot fat. Remove it. Now boil 4 cups of diced potatoes for 5 minutes; drain and add them to the hot fat. Add 2 cups of boiling water and simmer 5 more minutes. (Phil says he doesn't know why his aunt drained them and used fresh water except to remove the starch, which seems reasonable.) Add the fish and fish water and simmer 10 minutes, then add pork scraps, onion, 1 stick of butter, and 1 quart of scalded milk. Heat, but do not let it boil or the milk will curdle. When hot (takes just a few minutes), stir in ½ pint of cream. Serve in hot soup bowls with chowder crackers. As to how many it serves, you will have to find out. It depends on whether two bowls apiece is enough or your guests want three!

Phil is a charter-boat fisherman and his boat is called *Whitecap*. I like that better than *Lulu May* or *Annie*. It would be a disaster if anyone had ever named a boat *Gladys* for me, but I can imagine how it must feel to be so honored. Sometimes when I'm at the Cape I take Holly and go to Rock Harbor when the boats come in at high tide and it happens to be sunset. All boats are beautiful, I think, even battered old derelicts; but these rugged, powerful craft have a grace which comes from being perfectly constructed for their destiny.

Speaking of Cape Cod, Henry Beston's *The Outermost House* is now in paperback and everyone should have it. I've been rereading *The House on Nauset Marsh*, by Dr. Wyman Richardson, and getting extra copies for Christmas gifts, along with Hal Borland's *Countryman*. (I wish Hal were twins, getting out two books at once.) Sally Carrighar's *Wild Heritage* is fine reading, and for anyone with time *Queen Victoria* is a must.

My Cape Codder friend Clayton Horton tells me that one time a boat got stranded on the great beach near the Outermost House and the crew were trying desperately to get her off. They marked her sides with chalk so they could see whether they were really making headway or not. The Captain, bent over and heaving away, lost his pencil in the surf, and Henry waded out, up to his armpits, and rescued it from the water. It was, said Clayton, a small pencil. It is an endearing anecdote. Was it because Henry was thrifty or because a pencil was a writer's tool? I wonder.

The October air is crisp and clean; it's good picnic weather. A good many articles are being written about the passion for eating outdoors that has overwhelmed our country. With fine push-button kitchens full of labor-saving devices, what do we do? We pack a basket and go out. Or we coax a reluctant fire in a grill and work our heads off to have a meal that could be done in jig time in a modern range with a timer oven. However, this does not seem silly to me. My mother might be called a pioneer eater-outer, for we ate outside in the back yard, sitting on camp stools.

Sometimes we fared farther afield; then Father took a hatchet and an ax and just cut the material for the fire wherever we stopped. Wisconsin in those days was a wild and lovely land and very little of it was posted. Nobody worried about picnickers, who were few and far between. Father always built a massive fire, enough to barbecue an ox, and then took hours putting it out. He lugged water from the trout stream or lake and drowned it, then he dug up dirt and buried it, and then he wet it down again. And after we were settled in the car, he would bound out and go back, just to be sure.

The fire itself was used chiefly for the big coffeepot and for hamburgers. Mama brought fried chicken, deviled eggs, sliced baked ham, sandwiches, and so on, all ready to eat.

In season, of course, we had corn, which Father roasted until it was black. Sometimes we had an all-day picnic with the family doctor (he had one day off every few months). Then we played horseshoes and charades and finished the day with a light snack of homemade bread, cheese, and green apple pie. And so home, as Mr. Pepys says, and to bed.

What I chiefly remember about those innocent childhood days is the absence of fear. I was afraid of just two things, copperheads and Father when he was angry. Now, fear is a companion of us all. When the sonic boom crackles the old windowpanes in this house that has stood steadfast for almost three hundred years, I wonder. And when the jet planes thunder over, I look up and wonder again. When I turn the radio on, I brace myself for what has happened in the past twelve hours. We grow accustomed to this, but I am sorry for it.

When I consider how brief our stay on earth is, it seems a pity to waste any of it because of fear. I think of the phrase, "For God so loved the world . . . ," and I think we very much need more of that all-encompassing love for our fellow man.

So many things can present problems. Even in my village, the quiet has been disturbed. A battle developed over whether to let a group of promoters build a housing project which would change our rural area to a busy town. Those of us who care about the countryside were heartsick. Those who wanted added income for the town were for it, and town meetings were bitter and cruel. It is probably as well that I was not there for the most violent struggle. (I made my one and only speech at town meeting when the German Bund had secretly bought up a nice piece of land and begun erecting a youth camp. At that time my natural shyness vanished in a puff of words. But the speech that finished the Bund was made by a quiet-voiced Yankee who said simply, "We got along without you all these years, guess we don't need you now—or your money either.") This will be a long battle, and I dare say the promoters will win in the end. But the quiet hills and valleys and my beloved village will be changed. Woods will be laid waste as crackerboxes spring up overnight, and eventually Southbury will be just another suburb of a big city.

Often people write to me asking just when fall color is at its best in New England. It varies: it can be early and soon or very late. Often a few trees stay green as summer while the rest are ablaze. I often wish I were a naturalist like Hal Borland, and I also wish I were a geologist as my father was. I would like to understand the processes of nature as much as anyone can and to know the history of the earth. Of course no one can know enough about any field, but I think our education lacks much.

It is possible to do as I did—go to college, graduate, go on for an M.A.—and be woefully ignorant of so much, and such important matters. I wish I had had just a small bit of physics, even though I should have undoubtedly failed. Science is astonishing to me—now we can orbit the earth and put spacecraft on the moon eventually. But I am full of questions that do not get answered. Then there is history. I took one whole year on the Reformation and gulped it like a hungry puppy—but that isn't a wide knowledge of history by any means.

Languages are another thing. I believe children should begin at least one foreign language in the early grades, when it is so easy for them to learn. I had German in high school and was able to read a few of the German classics, but I never knew a word of French until I went to college and then I didn't absorb it at all. Latin is basic, in my opinion, for it is the mother of all languages—or almost all. Properly taught, Latin is exciting, and if you take it all through high school it is a valuable tool the rest of your life. It is not a dead language at all, for a large percentage of our own words have Latin roots. When I meet a strange word, I can usually figure the meaning because there will be that Latin tucked in it.

I could list some other vital subjects, but there isn't, of course, time to take them all. But certainly, as the world grows more complex and life more intricate, we should take a long look at what our schools offer and work in a few more essentials along with spelling and arithmetic.

An encouraging note is the influx of adult education courses. Everything from accounting to rugmaking is available in some schools. This is a fine thing, for it serves two purposes: the acquiring of knowledge and an extension of the learning process.

As I drive to the village to buy some groceries I notice

men making windbreaks around the very old houses. Evergreen branches packed closely help keep the drafts out, and they also look festive. Dead leaves are used, too, with chicken wire to hold them in. Storm windows go on toward the end of the month and storm doors are hung. And on a still day, I hear the sound of axes up the hill, for the woodpiles must be high. The wood should be well seasoned, but for a holding fire I put one or two fairly green logs in along with the seasoned ones. I collect small fallen branches all year for kindling. They really should be tied in bundles, but I am not that kind of person. I toss them in cartons and fish them out in handfuls as needed.

Before I left the house, Ed Koch came to clean out the great chimney and he had his fancy blower. In the early days, the man of the house had to climb on the roof and hang long heavy chains down the flue and shake them. The clotted soot must have floated all over the house even with a quilt tacked over the opening. A good many old houses burned down because of chimney fires in those long-ago times. Evidently there was a fire at Stillmeadow once, for the lath in the upstairs closet is charred. It is a wonder so many houses survived, for putting out a fire with hand buckets of water lugged from a well was a rugged task.

I enjoy my drive to the market. "It's a beautiful day!" I say to Eleanor Hoxie, who is at the check-out.

"Beautiful," she says. She is beautiful herself, in a lilac skirt and sweater. She has shining eyes and a lovely smile and is as always fresh as a meadow violet.

"The swamp," I say. "I wish you would come and look at it."

Now to a Southerner with flowing, easy speech, this wouldn't sound like much. But to New Englanders, it sounds just right. We are sharing our feelings about the beauty of autumn, though we don't use many words to do it. I go over to the meat counter where Louie is sharpening a murderous-looking knife.

"How are you?" I ask.

"Can't complain," he says. "Lovely day."

When I go home with the groceries, I bring some scarlet and gold leaves in so the house can share too. I used to knock myself out ironing, waxing, oiling, polishing them, but I gave up doing it. Now I just put the branches in a gray stone jug.

When at last they fade, I lay them gently in the great

fireplace. As I light the fire, small flames catch the leaves, and a spicy odor fills the room. The scent of dead leaves is another of the many things that can't be described. It is cool and musty and something else which may be the vanished sap. It evokes memories of walking in deep autumn woods in Wisconsin when I was growing up, and of bonfires celebrating the big homecoming football game, and of picnics by the Eight Mile Brook when the small children dropped their frankfurters in the smoky embers. Jill used to say I spent half my life inhaling the smells of everything from mint to macaroni and that I certainly had some hound inheritance.

Next to music, I think scents can evoke more feeling than anything else. Mama never used real perfume, for instance, but she used to tuck little lavender bags into her bureau with the petticoats and lacy camisoles, and she sometimes touched the tips of her rosy ears with lavender cologne. This made an impression on me even before I knew what the scent was. Now, when I gather dried lavender, I can almost feel her presence. She also used glycerin and rose water, and years after she died, I found a bottle in some country drugstore and took off the stopper and I was carried right back to my childhood.

Father always smelled of smoke and lawn grass and chalk. In the spring and summer he was always mowing the lawn at six in the morning when the grass was soaking and Mama and I were trying to sleep. Being a professor, he carried chalk dust in his trouser cuffs, under his collar, in his rusty hair. Sometimes he experimented with shaving lotion, which he sloshed on until we had to open the windows. He never did anything by halves. In hunting season he smelled of guns.

I suppose I am like those teatasters that spend their lives just tasting various teas, only I might be called a "smell taster." I like to pick up a piece of wood from the woodpile and smell it: every kind of tree has its own odor. I like to pick up a handful of freshly cut grass and sniff the rich green smell of the blades.

And when I go into a strange house and feel comfortable, I think part of it may be that the house smells of flowers and polish and cheese and chocolate milk shakes and cats and/or dogs and damp sneakers. A house that doesn't smell of anything frightens me; it's as if nobody lived there. A house should smell of living.

Occasionally someone has asked me how I could have dogs and cats all over the house, smelly and unsanitary as they are. Naturally I cannot speak for all breeds of dogs or all cats, but my first Irish setter smelled of ripening hayfields and I named him Timothy. My dearly loved golden cocker, Dark Honey, smelled like the sweet grass that Indians used to make baskets from. Newborn cocker puppies, I discovered, when we began to raise them, have a sweet milk-and-honey scent. My Siamese cat bore an odor of incense except when she helped herself to the fried chicken on the counter, and then she smelled largely of chicken (that is a good smell too). My Abyssinian also suggested incense burned in some forgotten temple, smoky and musty. And the Manx smelled of the outdoors, weeds in flower, mole burrows, and tomatoes (he hunted in the tomato rows). On shampoo days, of course, they all smelled of shampoo. We washed the cats in orange sacks, and the house smelled of drying fur for quite some time afterward.

I know a lot of people who never bother to enjoy the sense of smell we are endowed with, and I am sorry for them. It is rewarding to take time to savor this special sense. When it is raining too hard to go out, I enjoy opening a window and sniffing the rain-scented air. In winter, I often step out in a blizzard just to smell the snow. One might think it has no odor, but this isn't true. Snow has a pure, fresh smell—a distillation, if you will, of frozen air.

Among the flower fragrances, I think lilac is my favorite. When lilacs bloom, the air is "tangible"; it seems as if you could pick it in handfuls. It is rich but not cloying, heady but not intense as tropical odors are. White lilacs are more delicate, and white lilac is my favorite scent when it is bottled and sold. But if someone captured the scent of sugar maples in October in bottles I might prefer that!

I have a wise friend who really uses the appeal of smells in a practical way. She is a busy woman and sometimes gets home just a jump before her husband is due to arrive.

"I rush to the kitchen," she says, "without even taking my hat off, and I throw some bacon in the skillet. Then when Don opens the door, he smells something cooking and knows I am coping. If bacon is not on the supper menu, I save it for tomato and bacon sandwiches the next day." She adds thoughtfully, "It isn't that Don wants to run from the door to the dinner table. Few men do. I make up a martini before I go out and have his glass chilled in the refrigerator. I bring it to him, tell him I am so glad he is home. Then I get supper on. It works out."

While I firmly believe that marriage must be a partnership if it is to be a good one, I think women can do a few extras. An empty house with a note on the kitchen table about the casserole to put in the oven doesn't really "lift a man's forehead," as a Southern friend used to put it. And it is fine to be thrifty, but if the homemaker turns the thermostat down to 62 degrees as she leaves in the morning and the man of the house gets home first, his heart will not be warmed by the chilly air. It is better to spend the extra money and have a toasty warm house for him when he returns in the evening.

Almost everyone has ideas about modern marriage and the divorce rate and what is wrong. I know some very happily married people and have observed that small thoughtfulness shores up many a foundation. I have known a husband who drops a note in the laundry hamper along with his golf and gardening clothes. It says I LOVE YOU. That wife never has uttered a complaint about the washing and ironing.

It is part of a human being to want to be cherished, and cherished as an identity. During courting days, cherishing is 100 per cent. But often in the prosaic time that follows, mortgages and business and clubs and children take over the stage.

"Sometimes I think I don't know Bill any more," said a friend of mine one day. She didn't.

But the office secretary did. She gave her attention to Bill all day long (and she was paid for it, but never mind). She was also ready to join him for lunch or work overtime and have dinner at one of those romantic dimly lighted restaurants. This wasn't one of those marriages that magazines write about, with problems like alcoholism, miserliness, in-law difficulty, or some kind of persecution. It was just a drifting marriage.

Finally, both of them realized what was happening to them. Bill didn't want to wreck his marriage and Jane did love him, so they worked out a solution to the problem. They saved one night a week to be together. No matter what came up, friends and business associates learned that this night they were not available. After all, there are very few things that can't be attended to the next day. On their night they didn't dress up and go wining and dancing and dining.

"Acting like young lovers isn't going to help," said Jane. "We just need to give some time to each other."

Sometimes, in summer, they got a baby sitter and took pleasant drives around the countryside. They spent other evenings playing records they loved which had gathered dust for so long. On cool evenings they sat by the fire and popped corn and watched television. They even read aloud from their favorite books. And when the secretary got married, they gave her a handsome silver bowl.

Perhaps they water-skied, rode surfboards, went sailing, golfed, or played tennis. It doesn't really matter what they did; it was, I think, the sharing that counted.

"And we have a pact," Jane told me. "We do not discuss the children or the office. We talk about politics, government, religion, music, books. We talk about ourselves."

I like to think about these two, especially when I hear about two others who are being married for the fourth time even though they don't live in Hollywood! I don't mean to say I think all marriages are salvageable, for they are not. I only feel that a rather sizable proportion might be if they were worked at with half the dedication spent on most business partnerships (which after all are not as vital).

When the hunter's moon rises over the old orchard, it is the color of a fire opal. The Indians who named it are long gone, but I still find quartz arrowheads by the pond. As I go out with the cockers and Holly for a last walk about the yard at moonrise, I sometimes think I can see tall, dark figures walking leaf-light at the edge of the garden. Occasionally Teddy will sit back on his golden self and bark loudly, so I expect an Indian dog or two is there also. It reminds me that I do not own this piece of land, not even this house. I am, in a way, lent it for a time. The house belongs to a sturdy man who built it in 1690. The land wasn't his really, it was the Indians' home place before he came. We are all, I think, sojourners.

I reflect that nothing really ends, but grows into something new. The harvest is in and the leaves will all be down soon, but they enrich the ground, and new leaves will put forth tender green in spring, in the endless cycle of nature. Today is a part of time, a unit, but it evolved from yesterday and flows into tomorrow like a tide.

Sidonie Coryn

November

TEATIME comes early at Stillmeadow now. I hang the kettle over the embers, bring out the toasting fork, and open the sweet-clover honey.

In November the Stillmeadow road has done with summer and with gold and scarlet. But the sunny stillness and the haze that dreams over the woods tell me that Indian Summer has come. The *Old Farmer's Almanac* dares to set dates for its arrival and departure—November 13–20—but nature has her own schedule. Whenever it comes, though, the dogs and I bask in the balmy air, feeling just plain lazy, thinking of all kinds of reasons to put off the chores that await me. Perhaps Indian Summer is the opposite of Spring Fever!

When the air is blue with haze and smells of woodsmoke and the sun is gentle and dreamy; I sit on the terrace by the old well house and read, turning the pages slowly and most of the time just sitting.

There isn't really any such thing as summer reading, I

think, or winter reading; there is just reading. But I do think some poetry belongs especially to Indian Summer. I've been browsing through Robert Frost's *Collected Poems,* and what a delight it is. He was the great countryman poet, and this book should be in every household, well worn, as mine is. My Rupert Brooke is also worn and shabby, the pages are yellowing, and there is a good deal of underlining in it. Lines like

> My night shall be remembered for a star
> That outshone all the suns of all men's days

Or:

> And flowers themselves, that sway through sunny hours,
> Dreaming of moths that drink them under the moon. . . .

Now I don't really believe moths actually drink flowers— it certainly doesn't fit in with what I know of the moths I have met—but it is such pure beauty that it doesn't matter at all. It evokes magic.

Poetry should be shared, and I am sorry that reading aloud is so out of fashion nowadays. The very few friends I have that voluntarily ask me to read some poetry aloud are rarer than a narcissus in a snowbank. When I was young, I went around with a book of verse under my arm and just collared hapless classmates and *read* to them, but one cannot do that when one is adult!

Bittersweet hangs vermilion berries over the gray stone wall by the brook. Black alder burns into color by the pond.

There used to be a great deal of both bittersweet and alder, but passers-by have ruined most of it.

One autumn day a few years ago a carload of trippers stopped by the fence along Jeremy Swamp and began tearing whole bittersweet vines from the trees. Jill dashed out and down the road, her long legs doing a marathon. When she told them firmly but quietly that this was posted private property, two of the young men jeered and ripped down another whole vine. Jill flew back down the road, banged open the door, and reached for the Revolutionary musket sitting on the mantel. Now although Jill had more skills than any other woman I have ever known, she couldn't have hit the Town Hall with a good firearm. But off she charged with that musket and, as she approached the predators, they fell from the trees in a wild scramble, jumped into their car, and burned up the road escaping. The vines were ruined except for a few they hadn't had time to haul down.

I could imagine what they said as they reached the safety of the highway: "Madwoman," they must have said. "Going to kill us just for getting a few of them old berries. Crazy people out here in the wilds, just crazy."

I put on the coffeepot, on my usual theory that coffee is fine for fatigue, excitement, and shortness of breath (Jill's asthma wouldn't be improved by her charges up and down that hill).

When she came back, her face was white and she had torn her best shirt on some briers during the charge. She hung the musket in its proper place again and sank down on the sofa and tried to ease her breathing by holding her hands on her chest. "They didn't know it wasn't loaded," she said.

"If it had been, you might have blown your head off," I remarked.

Yes, the bittersweet was ruined but the vandals never came back. And now, as I put a few small twigs in a brown jug, I always smile, remembering Jill's defense of the home place. And sometimes I imagine the city people telling everyone the country was full of madwomen with guns.

Nonetheless, the habits of some American motorists are enough to discourage anyone. Around the first of December the Christmas trees Jill planted begin to diminish in number, and Steve and Olive, down the road, lost a number of big ones a few years ago.

In spring cars drive along the highway loaded with dogwood and azalea, both of which are on the conservation list. The fern pickers come to the woods, but for some reason, I do not mind them. I hear their voices, thin and clear, when I wake in the morning. The fern pickers climb the craggy places at the upper end of my land, and the going is rough there. I rather like to think the ferns, cool and dark, will reach the city by noon and perhaps carry the scent of deep woods to the smog-deep city streets. The ferns are stolen, true, but the supply is inexhaustible, so far as I know. Somehow it is not like wrenching up the bittersweet or digging the azaleas.

The days grow colder, clouds scud on gray skies, long

rains and early twilights precede the real winter. Color it gray. But how we welcome the rain after the droughts of summer.

"Well's filling up," says Joe. "Pond's getting high."

"Glad it's rain and not the white stuff," says George at the market. "Hope we'll have a time yet before we get out the shovels."

Once a reader of one of my books wrote and complained because I never mentioned rain and was the sun always shining at Stillmeadow? I used to purely hate rain. But I discovered it, in an odd way. One day some years ago heavy downpours kept me indoors, and, for once, I was not working. I sat and watched the rain for an hour. Every rain is different, I found out, and each has its own personality. Some falls thick and heavy (like Somerset Maugham's rain), and some slants until it is almost horizontal. Spring rains tend to be quick, as if they had to hurry and let the sun come out. The rain during a strong hurricane is like having a river suddenly change its natural course and try to rush right through the house. It bounces on the window sills and is loud as hail. Perhaps you think raindrops should be colorless, or at least always the same, but a hurricane rain is dark and an April rain is silvery. November rain is the color of pewter.

Once I really gave myself up to thinking about rain, I began to like it. (I admit the constant water shortages in New England helped.) Now, there is no sound sweeter than the sudden beat of rain at midnight after a long, dry spell. Wind usually comes with it in New England, so the impact is hard on the old glass panes. A really sturdy nor'easter sends water under the back door. We often have three-day rains, but what one broadcaster in Boston calls "rain showers" are more likely. Then in the morning the washed earth shines as if it had been polished. When I go out, I find a few late buds are opening that escaped the black frost. It is like finding pearls in an oyster.

I am told man can subsist an incredible length of time with no food, but without water he must die. Perhaps this is a heritage from primordial times when, if we believe the scientists, life began in the seas. Our bodies still have a large water content; although we walk on land, the tie is still between us and the seas. I think it is so with the earth. Without water, there would be only desert sand blowing in the wind. So the long, dark rains are life itself to my valley.

When it isn't raining, the air is damp and smells deliciously of fallen leaves and garden fires. It is safe, at last, to burn cornstalks and pruned debris and anything which has harbored blight or pests. But the leaves go in the compost pile or are used as mulch. "Waste not, want not" is the rule with countryfolk. And also, if you take from the land you must give back to it.

The compost heap is part of country back yards and needs only sprinklings of lime now and then between layers of grass clippings, vegetable peelings, and so on. I well remember our first one.

"I am starting a compost pile," announced Jill one fall morning. "And I've found just the place."

She had, too. It was the base of a departed silo, a large, circular cement and stone affair, almost as deep as a well. As I peered into it, I suggested it would make a lovely garden pool—fish and waterlilies and things, I said.

"Can't make a garden pool next to the barn," said Jill.

For two seasons she worked on the compost heap and it was a fine one. There was just one trouble: in order to get anything out of it, you needed a steam shovel. Eventually she managed to shovel out the top foot, and that was all. From then on, our compost pile was above ground, in the vegetable garden, and while it did not look pretty at least it was available.

Now that the small ones will be spending more time indoors, one important task before the family arrives for the week end is to check the medicines as well as anything in household use that could be lethal swallowed or even just tipped with a rosy tongue. I keep all of the dog medications in a separate box, labeled (for the grownups) and tucked away on a high shelf. As I sort it, I think wistfully of the wonderful hormone-plus pills that Holly now takes. It is a temptation to see what they would do for me—but I resist.

For the various vitamins and pills that I am supposed to take, I finally found a solution. They come in plastic-topped bottles and I took one of those markers and initialed the caps in large black letters. This saves reading the label three times (as a nurse once recommended) and means I am not likely to take two of what I am to take ONE of. I assemble the formidable array in round plastic containers that can be raised to a high spot before the young fry comes. I can just see Betsy deciding to take one of those violet pills, the color is so pretty. At her age arthritis is no problem, but the pill might be!

There are so many accidents from carelessness with pills and medicines that I am astonished to keep on hearing about a three-year-old who ate a whole bottle of something or other while Mother was getting breakfast. Medicines, from thyroid to aspirin, should be locked up.

Then there are pretty bottles of softeners, cleansers, pink liquid detergents. I *think* Betsy is now too mature to sample them, but I am not sure. It is a good thing for a parent to go through the house and be sure nothing is at hand that could be a disaster. Betsy can go on eating dog biscuits, but that's different.

I also think matches should not be too easy to pick up. A very small child may watch adults strike matches every now and then all day and think it would be such fun to strike one. Some severe burns have resulted from this.

I finish by putting the most valuable pieces of milk glass out of the way. A special bit of milk glass like the hand with the green stone on one finger represents years of search and would break as easily as a soap bubble. I don't think it a good idea for children to live in a No–No–No world when it can be avoided. I still regret the time on the Cape one summer when Anne came up from the beach with her arms full of dripping salty seaweed which she proposed to bring in just as I put the vacuum cleaner away. I did say NO very firmly, and her rose-petal face crumpled up and two large tears rolled down her cheeks.

"Gramma won't let me bring it in!" she reported to her father.

So poor Curt had to take her on a special jaunt while the ache wore off. My only defense was that I could not drag that cleaner around one more inch and company was dropping in and I ached too, all over. But I should have figured on this sodden mess being just what some rabbit needed for a nest and helped her find a nice place under the rose bushes where she could place her sea treasure.

Of course I believe in discipline, for the results of permissive upbringing can be terrifying in the teen ages. But discipline should have a reason which the child accepts and not seem just another tyrannical act on the part of a large, looming grownup. And why reject an armful of seaweed? No sense at all.

I naturally feel my grandchildren and Jill's are unusually well mannered and sensible. As a completely objective observer, I find them exceptional, but then so were their parents!

Sometimes in a store I hear a mother screaming at a small boy and watch him cringe, and I use all of my restraint not to turn and screech at *her*. I know what must go on at home, if this happens out in public. I know it is hard to shop with a small child, but even so. . . .

Every few years I am suddenly reminded that I have no winter wardrobe. I discover my ten-year-old coat is shabby at the cuffs, too long, and fuzzy around the bottom. My dresses are few and hang limp on the hangers—obviously they have had it. So finally I talk myself into shopping, and New Haven seems a million miles away. I cannot understand women who "adore shopping." I have a friend who can spend a whole day looking for a hat. I never wear hats. I gave away the ones I had a long time ago. When it snows, I tie one of those slippery things on my head. And I never go to a formal affair, so I only need casual clothes, easy to work in, easy to run in and out in.

When it's possible to do so, I go to my favorite shop on the Cape where a dear friend meets me at the door, looking like a gentle edition of *Vogue* but welcoming me in my shabby costume as if it were quite the thing.

"Dorothy, I want a coat," I say. "Not too heavy, preferably blue."

"Well, would you like something like this?" She brings out a not-too-heavy blue coat.

"That's fine," I say. "I'll take it."

"But let me show you one or two others—" she pleads.

"This is just fine," I assure her. "I also need a soft dress, preferably blue."

"This one just came in," she says, patient as always, "and it is the color you want—will you try it on?"

"Must I?"

"I think you'd better. And I'll find a few more to try."

"I know this will be just right," I say hurriedly.

In the end I usually spend twenty minutes, leaving her a

little limp but resigned, because nobody else shops this way.

I always wear flat shoes, and cannot help deploring the pumps my daughter wears with what look like hatpins for heels. I point to the pair I have on and tell the shoe clerk I want the same shoes, only new and unspotted. This is not so easy, for no manufacturer ever seems willing to repeat an ideal shoe. I have learned if I really thoroughly like a certain last and leather, I should take three pairs because I shall not see their like again.

I always feel a pang when I discard some faithful old pair of shoes and work my feet into some strange new type. I wonder whether the manufacturers really are right in thinking women never want the same kind of thing twice? Changing styles every season, twice a season at times, may not really be as important as they think.

British raincoats, I am glad to say, are the same now as when I was growing up. My current British raincoat resembles the first one I ever had, except it is now called London Mist and I forget what they called it then. London Fog?

In November we remember John Fitzgerald Kennedy. Not that he is unremembered during the rest of the year, for it seems to me that in my time no man has remained in the consciousness of America, and perhaps the world, as President Kennedy has. The legend has not died; the eternal flame burns over the grave of this man. In a few short years he wrote his signature strong and vital on the pages of history. And it is significant that this American was honored at Runnymede.

I remember only too well the day he was assassinated. A group of close friends was to have tea at Yvonne's in her beautiful house by the sea on Cape Cod. Early in the day, my dear neighbor Millie had come to help me sort and pack for the trip back to Stillmeadow. We had the radio on as we flung coats and dresses in heaps on the bed. I was standing in the closet when the first news came, and suddenly it was as if the darkness of the closet enlarged and spread over the whole earth.

Millie and I sat down in the living room and said not a word. We just sat in a dreadful paralysis, trying to hope and knowing immediately there was no hope. After a time Millie brought me a cup of hot black coffee.

"Better drink this," she said.

We did no more work that day. Millie went home to be there when Ed came in from work. "He won't know," she said.

Then around five I called Ted, another friend. "We won't be having tea today," I told him.

"Yvonne says we had better be together," he said in a queer, flat voice.

When I went out, the late sun was shining and there was no wind. A bevy of quail feeding on the lawn scattered. A rabbit sat and looked at me with that blank stare Cape rabbits have. Holly came from the beach dripping sand and seaweed. The world is still here, I thought, in sheer amazement.

NOVEMBER

At Yvonne's we sat silently. We drank the hot fragrant tea; the cups rattled loudly in the fragile saucers. I held mine with both hands because I could not stop shaking. The village priest was there and he managed some conversation in a brave attempt to rouse us from shock, but I can't recall a word he said except it had to do with travel. The light ebbed and that day, too, ended. When we said good-by, we all clung to one another as if we might shelter ourselves. Yvonne looked as if her face were carved from marble. She is one of the most beautiful women I have known, with wide-set sea-gray eyes, a mobile fine mouth, and softly swept-back hair. She is usually so animated, you feel lights are flashing all over the room. That afternoon she might have been a figure on a Renaissance tomb.

I stayed up all night but fell asleep around dawn. When I awoke, I had that first feeling that it was a dream—it was not true at all. On Sunday I turned on the television just in time to see Oswald shot. The rest of the day people telephoned and wandered in and out, and by Monday most of us tried to take up the ordinary tasks we had to do. The effect of insupportable shock affects people differently. Some find it easier to bear if they can blame somebody, so this had to be the fault of the F.B.I., the Dallas police, the C.I.A. It was the fault of the government that allowed this man to ride around insufficiently protected in a world of unbalanced men, and it was somebody's fault that Oswald was running around buying mail-order murder weapons.

I can never find comfort in blame, although it is quite obvious that this tragedy evidenced carelessness somewhere by somebody. But it is a handy crutch for some people. And hindsight often reveals what foresight has not.

I think we as a nation are often casual and smug. We think, "It couldn't happen here." Possibly this is better than walking in fear, but there should be a middle road.

As each Thanksgiving comes, I think we can be thankful that John Fitzgerald Kennedy was given to his country even for so brief a time. And thankful not only for his leadership but because he and his wife brought back grace and elegance to the White House along with an appreciation of art and poetry and music. In an industrial society, these need cherishing, and for a time they were.

One morning I wake up and all my little summertime friends have flown away. At the feeder, chickadees, nuthatches, blue jays, and woodpeckers are bustling about, reminding me of returned vacationers settling in after a long time away. With the snow come the juncoes—often called snowbirds—small, trim cloud-gray birds, with pearl-pink bills and faintly pink breasts. They arrive in flocks and are ground feeders. One thing puzzles me. Whenever I picked up Robert, the quail who lived with Dr. and Mrs. Kienzle on the Cape, I noticed that her tiny feet were cold as icicles; but they warmed up quickly if she remained in my hand. Therefore, I figure, the circulation of other birds should be the same. So why don't the juncoes' feet freeze as these little birds hop around in the snow?

I also wonder why delicate songbirds don't migrate in

winter, or hibernate. Their normal temperature, I'm told, is 101 degrees (and we think we're ill when we have that much of a temperature). The chickadees will fly to the feeder in a driving snowstorm and chatter cheerfully as they crack sunflower seeds, while I hunt up my snow boots and mittens before venturing outside.

The relationship between birds and man can be a rewarding one, for even the shyest of them respond to gestures of friendship. The distance between my little visitors and me has been bridged by the offering of sunflower seeds, chick-feed, raisins, suet cakes, and bread crumbs. As I talk softly, I am answered by the fluttering of wings and a dipping toward my hands. I cannot help thinking that barriers between people could also be bridged by the extending of an open hand.

I once had an unusual experience when I was on Cape Cod. For the first time in my life I saw Canada geese at close range. Stately and majestic, they moved across the salt pond below my window, seven of them, in uneven formation. They were grayish, with white neck markings that looked like scarves which they'd tied under their chins. They weighed, I thought, eight pounds or more. They had evidently wintered in the duck pond behind the big pond where the eelgrass is plentiful and there is plenty of shelter.

They stopped under my windows to feed in the shallows, dipping and lifting their heads on their long, curving necks. Then the leader mounted guard on the shingle and the rest *took baths!* They dipped heads deep in water, flung the drops over their breasts and backs, and preened their feathers. This took some time, and then I think someone else took over so the leader could have his bath. The rest moved onto the shingle where the tide stirred the edges of the seaweed and spread great wings wide and waved them slowly up and down, obviously happy in the sunshine. Finally they nestled flat in the eelgrass. The leader was back guarding by now and kept his shiny eye scanning the land and water on all sides.

Since they had been swimming for almost three hours and were half submerged while feeding, I thought the baths were rather gilding the lily. But this was their routine, and after resting half an hour they slipped silently into the water and swam back to the inlet and vanished.

I shall never forget the wonder I felt. Subsequently, my neighbor Bobby scrambled his way around to the duck pond and reported he saw several goslings and they were "out of this world."

It is hard to understand why any man would want to shoot these "honkers" as they call them, but killing is not my dish.

When the children come for Thanksgiving, out comes the big roaster. Dinner is traditional, including fluffy turnips, cranberry sauce, giblet gravy, mashed potatoes. We do not, however, have the mince and apple pies. This is a sign of the times, for the children count calories and prefer to use them up on the main dinner. The small ones have dishes of ice cream while the adults have a fruit bowl, cheese, and crackers.

Toward evening, everyone is ready for cold turkey and thinly sliced dressing for sandwiches. It is self-service, for Mama is through for the day! Later we get out the corn popper and a bowl of apples, in case anyone is starving. We like corn popped in a rusty old popper from the early days, shaken back and forth over the embers in the fireplace. I use part oil and part butter and more salt than anyone would believe. My feeling is the oil spreads the butter more evenly —but this may be another of my notions.

It is a happy holiday and a reminder that we owe thanks to the forefathers who struggled in the alien land to find a foothold and establish a community. I do not think for a moment we had the right to displace the Indians—this is a black mark on our history and still is—nevertheless, the Pilgrims were refugees in a way, fleeing for religious liberty (but they imposed their religions on others afterward). History is nothing if not contradictory and confusing to me.

When Thanksgiving is over, Christmas is hard at hand—in fact I wish, at times, there could be just one more week between them. I have for years and years promised myself that I would plan so as to be fresh and rested when Christmas comes, but it seems I have just gotten the turkey soup frozen (How Don loves that soup "with things in it") when it is time to put up the tree.

I remember when turkey was a once-in-a-year dinner. It symbolized Thanksgiving. Ham was for Easter, along with eggs cooked in fancy ways. Roast beef and Yorkshire pudding meant Christmas in our house when I was growing up, or stuffed goose when Mama could get it.

Our turkey came to town from a farm near Black Creek, I believe, and I stood around waiting to see Father bring it in the house. Then that delicious smell of sage and onion and savory filled the house as Mama stuffed his majesty and tucked him in the gas oven (allowing plenty of time for the gas to die down around suppertime as it always did).

We were in Wisconsin and the relatives in New England, so a family gathering was out of the question, but Mama had a houseful, as usual—the family doctor and his wife, a couple of homesick students from the college, a couple of single members of the faculty. All the leaves were put in the big mahogany table and the great lace cloth laid on. Father always said a hurried gruff blessing, for it embarrassed him to talk publicly to God. He addressed Him in private rather as one equal to another, but at the dinner table he flushed and ran the words together.

Nowadays turkey is so available it is no longer a seasonal treat. At times I am sorry it is so common, for that first thrill of seeing it on Thanksgiving morning is gone. The grandchildren accept turkey as just another good meal. I won't go so far as to say it should be restricted to holidays, but a few things should still be rare treats, I think. Of course it always is a treat to me because, since I live alone, the only turkey I meet is when the children assemble for a week end or a holiday. One person, even with the help of an Irish and cockers, cannot undertake even a small turkey. The halfturkeys now available are fine for apartment dwellers but still too much for me.

November for me is a good time for meditation. As I watch the violet twilight casting shadows over the valley, I think what a long way we have come since the post riders spurred their horses down from Boston and our church bell rang out and everyone gathered to hear the news of Concord and Lexington. It took, I believe, two days for word to reach here. Today, we see and hear about events almost as they are happening!

The early years of our country were hard and bitter, and

we have seen many such since. The course of history is dark and bloody more often than not. But I believe with all my heart that there is a hard core of belief in individual rights in our country, and a faith in the democratic way of life. We do not doubt that these are worth preserving at any cost, not only for ourselves but for our children.

I just wish our elections had more dignity. After all, it isn't the party with the most balloons and buttons, the loudest cheering sections and biggest signs at conventions that may provide responsible government. I think we should educate children from the first grade on to have more interest in political affairs. And our whole system of electing a President should be studied and changed, if necessary, so that elections can take place in a practical, economical manner.

In a world of turmoil, where poverty and prejudice still exist, where fathers and sons and sweethearts and husbands are fighting in steaming jungles far away, I am thankful for so very much. No voice is raised in hatred in my household. Footsteps sound gently on the threshold, with no echo of nailed boots. The grandchildren walk and play without fear. The dogs settle on the wide hearth and doze into a warm, comfortable sleep. The steady glow of friendship warms me daily: Joe brings me a new load of firewood; Erma takes me to the dentist in the next town so that I won't have to go alone; Steve and Wilma bring me some special country sausage, which they get from the South.

There are gay evenings with Wilma and Willie, and Tommy shows me how to work his tape recorder; dinners with Millie and Ed after we watch a thrilling football game; long afternoons with Barbara and Slim, during which we sip coffee and talk about everything from recipes to literature. There are sunset drives with my friend Faith Baldwin; fireside games of Scrabble with Helen Beals; hamburgers and home-baked beans with Helen and Vicky; Joan Baez records with Bobby Gibson, with cheese and crackers and a bowl of fruit at hand. These are simple things, but to me they are most precious. And as I recall each one, November's beaver moon shines brighter than ever and I know that love and friendship, hearth fires, and faith are indeed gifts to be thankful for and to treasure always.

December

WINTER sifts down on Stillmeadow with the falling snow. The snowfall gives a strange impermanence to the countryside, blurring the far hills, silvering the pond, tipping the mailbox with ermine. The air itself seems silver-white. There is a lovely feeling when the world turns white. But there is also a sadness as the last page of the calendar appears. This is the natural condition of man, I think, to be reluctant to let go of the known and face toward the unknown.

A friend in California writes that she worries about my cockers and the Irish when the cold weather comes. This makes me realize that, to people who never know winter, it is natural to worry. Actually the dogs are better off in winter than in summer. I worry about them during the hot breathless days in August. By now they have their heavier fur coats.

I go to the village earlier in the afternoon now that it gets dark so early. Also, the ice may have melted a bit on the road and the wind is less cutting. I learned this the time I went late with Holly and drove carefully up the hill, only to get stuck right in front of my own mailbox just three feet away from a nice bare spot on the road. There was not a soul anywhere within sight or sound, and I figured out it might well be the next morning before anyone came down Jeremy Swamp Road (it is not a busy road at any time).

I tried rocking back and forth—and now advise others that it may only make things worse. I tried racing the motor under the misapprehension that the heat of the car might melt some of the ice. Then I had to open all the windows so that Holly and I could breathe. I got out and looked for dead branches along the swamp, but if that swamp had been combed there couldn't have been less sign of a twig.

Then I sat and thought. An agile person would simply get out and hike a mile or so to reach a phone and call for help, I told Holly. However, since I have arthritis, this did not seem like a good idea.

"Whatever you do, dear, don't fall," were the words my doctor had spoken to me at the last session. But how could I be sure I wouldn't slip on that ice even as the car did? There was the car, big, powerful creature, stuck flat and helpless.

Finally I got Holly's army blanket out from under her and laid it carefully under the left rear wheel, got in, backed over it, and lo, we were off! The blanket wasn't much good anyway, I told Holly, who objected. I felt as Sir Walter Raleigh must have when he flung his jeweled cloak under

Queen Elizabeth's feet that muddy day in olde England.

(My only other accident with the car was when the push-button window flew up on its own and trapped my hand while I was fiddling with it. That day, Bobby Gibson came along and got me unwound before the bones cracked. Push-button windows are a joy, but it is not a good idea to leave one hand on the top of the glass if the button sticks momentarily.)

The Christmas catalogues start arriving in the mail. They are gay and glittering, and they list everything from mechanical dolls to mink toothbrushes. So much work has gone into the making of them that it is a pity they are so transient. Nothing is deader than last year's Christmas catalogues. All the glow and glitter should be used for something, I think, whether you buy the jeweled scarves and men's silk lounging robes or not.

I love to go through the catalogues and, yes, I do order things for the children—a pinky-soft robe for Muffin, mittens for Anne, and a few things for the grownups. But I remember when we first moved to Stillmeadow, there were two catalogues everyone lived by, aside from the seed catalogues. Some of the neighbors shopped via Sears Roebuck, some via Montgomery Ward. And we swapped catalogues, which was a delightful custom. "I'll bring you over Sears, and may I borrow Montgomery?"

Something very special happens in December. As Christmas cards and notes arrive, I step briefly from my own life into the lives of people who are dear to me, but far away. And, strangely, I move back in time with old friends. I am glad to know that Charlotte has another grandchild, but I see her as a girl with wind-tossed hair and laughter like golden bells. I am back in the parlor (for we had parlors in my small town), and she is playing by ear on a shiny upright piano. She is always playing "Maple Leaf Rag" because that is what I always ask for. It is good news that Harry has built a new house, but I see him again as a tall, long-legged boy covered with mud and making a touchdown on the football field. Peg is in California; the children are grown up. But I think of the long violet twilights when she walked home with me and then I walked home with her and then she walked home with me and then we both were roundly scolded by our parents for being late to supper.

As the greeting cards arrive, I put them on two of the mantels, in the corner cupboard where I keep the milk glass, and on the bookshelves. During this festive season I can pause in my daily rounds as the gay Christmas tidings on each card catch my eye.

The whole valley begins to take on a holiday appearance as December goes along. The giant pine at the village center glows with lights. Christmas wreaths blossom on every door. George decorates the market, and Green's store looks like a Christmas party. The post office is piled so high with packages that I can barely see the heads of the postal workers. No window is without a string of lights, a sprig of green, or a glitter of tinsel.

But I think I must be the first person in the village to put up Christmas trimmings. Erma helps me decorate Stillmeadow with mistletoe, holly, and pine branches, which add a green, spicy touch to the old house. Christmas candles brighten the wide window ledges, but I never put them on the tree, for I am afraid they might start a fire. Bowls of fruit and nuts appear—temporary decorations, for the children start munching and cracking as soon as they arrive for the holiday. The bowl on the coffee bench has to be refilled several times a day.

When it is time to put up the tree, out come the cherished ornaments that have survived a Siamese, a good many cocker puppies, the waving tails of several Irish setters, and various small children who couldn't resist patting shiny balls. Some even decided that a tree was for climbing! We always put our tree in the front living room, and as the gaily wrapped presents are ready they go under it.

I hope Christmas gifts never go out of style, for they are evidence of loving and caring, which all of us need. I love the excitement that accompanies the opening of boxes—the rustle of tissue paper, the exclamations of surprise and delight, the stepping over toy trains and stuffed toys and educational blocks, the wallet and tie clasp and four ties, the dainty slip and leather gloves and fragrant colognes in pretty bottles. I know some people gladly settle for money, but how prosaic that is! Gifts may be lavish, they may be simple, but it is so nice to be remembered.

I think, on the whole, books make the most satisfying presents. A fine book is a lifelong friend. Time does not stale it, it becomes dearer. In happy hours it is a delight; in time of sorrow, a comfort. I like to give Hal Borland's *Sundial of the Seasons* or *This Hill, This Valley* to friends who didn't get them before. My son-in-law Curt, who shares my love of poetry, will enjoy Aileen Ward's excellent book *John Keats: The Making of a Poet*. For fiction, Faith Baldwin's book, *The Lonely Man,* combines her magic storytelling with a good deal of wisdom and understanding. *The Story of the Cat at the Manger* by Rouben Mamoulian goes to both children and adults. It is moving and lovely; the illustrations a joy. James Gould Cozzens's book of short stories is the right gift for those who appreciate the best. I have not found a book recently that made me laugh out loud, and I am sorry about this. In this serious age, we need humor. Some I have read are funny part of the way, but how I miss something like James Thurber's "The Night the Bed Fell on Father!" Most humorists seem to be self-conscious and trying so hard. Thurber was like a spring, bubbling freshly.

There is, I think, a special bond between people who like the same books. It is a sharing rather like the sharing of favorite music. How happy I am when I find someone who appreciates Beverley Nichols and has managed to get one of his books about his various adventures in English country living. They were not always easy to come by in this country, but a half-dozen or so have been published here in the past few years. The test of a good book is that you want to read it again. I read Beverley Nichols once a year. But I have some friends who would prefer serious biography, which I also enjoy. I found Catherine Drinker Bowen's *Francis Bacon, The Temper of a Man,* a fascinating book, and it usually appears on my list of books for special people.

Records make excellent gifts too, for there's something to suit everyone's taste in music. For folksong lovers, there are the recordings of Joan Baez, Harry Belafonte, the Kingston Trio, and lots of others. Most people like to have albums of hit musicals in their record collections, and the choice is wide. Personally, I like any symphony conducted by Leonard Bernstein. Some albums cannot be played as background to conversation; they must be listened to. Others can be enjoyed while you're talking, munching Winesap apples, or popping corn in the fireplace.

The best gifts are not tangible, after all; nor do they come exclusively at Christmastime. My greatest Christmas gift came one summer on Cape Cod. It was a present from Dr. Bernstein and it was Holly coming out of the hospital after an emergency operation. Dr. Bernstein led her out on her leash. "Here's your girl," he said. I could hear all the stars singing that night.

Another very special gift I received one spring came from my friend Margaret. She went to a place in her woods and gathered a bouquet of arbutus for me. (Arbutus has mostly vanished and is on the conservation list but this was her own arbutus.) The delicate pearl-pink blossoms and shiny polished leaves were beautiful, and surely no scent is as delectable. But more than that, they made me think of time long past when my first love used to go to the lumber camps to work during school vacations. He was never a letter writer, but always I would get a bouquet of arbutus from the north woods, packed in wet moss in a shoe box. Margaret had no way of knowing she was giving me a cherished memory with her bouquet. She just said she thought I might like to know someone loved me! She caught a frightful case of poison ivy picking that arbutus, but she said she enjoyed being in the woods anyway.

Yes, the true spirit of Christmas is an all-year affair, and I expect the light of the Christmas star spills over into the coming year. The day may yet come when it also spills over the nations of the world, and we shall put away the missiles and do something nice and peaceful with atoms.

Christmas Eve is an important occasion for me. We sit around the fireplace talking about the past and the future. The tree glows softly in the light of the candles on the trestle table. Our voices join in the singing of carols, and in this uneasy world I find faith anew. Music, I think, is the basic art. It speaks to all in a language of its own. Nobody has to translate it; it requires only listening to. The words of the carols are beautiful, but even without them the message is clear. The power of love, the true significance of good will, shine forth with greater meaning at this holy time. The Babe born in that manger in Bethlehem was indeed the Prince of Peace and is so still.

I used to read Dickens' *A Christmas Carol* aloud when the children were growing up. I know it by heart because it was read to me every year when I was a child, and I feel it is a link between the generations. Nowadays, however, the very young make this sort of reading almost impossible. Even after they are tucked into bed they want a drink of water, or their go-to-sleep toy has fallen out of the crib, or can they stay up just five more minutes, or SOMETHING.

When the little ones are finally asleep, I have a chance to look at the three grownup children: my daughter and Jill's son and daughter. How beautiful to me they are. Time is a curious thing. They have not changed so very much, even though they have traveled far since the time they were asking for a drink of water at bedtime. How proud I am of them!

When everybody has gone to bed, I sit a few moments in the now-quiet house, watching the embers fade into ash, thinking how fortunate Stillmeadow is to have small feet still pattering around on the old oak floors. Inevitably, as I turn out the lights, Connie comes softly down the stairs.

"I just wanted to say what a lovely Christmas Eve this has been, Mama," she whispers. And this, of course, is the best present of all.

Holiday breakfasts at Stillmeadow are traditionally festive. I abandon my usual soft-boiled egg for pancakes with golden maple syrup and crisp, tiny sausages. Or creamed finnan haddie, which was Jill's favorite dish and which her son fixes for us now. Or corned beef hash, for a change.

And on New Year's Day, I fix broiled scallops for the children. I preheat the broiler and spread the scallops on a shallow baking pan; then I pour melted butter or margarine over the scallops and season with freshly ground pepper and seasoned salt. I broil them about three minutes, sprinkle with lemon juice (I like the new juice in plastic containers), and broil a minute or so more. I shake the pan once or twice. I serve them on toast wedges with lemon butter. Fried scallops are more often served, but I like the delicate flavor of the broiled ones.

In my childhood, New England breakfasts were robust, to say the least. At Uncle Walter's we had baked beans and codfish cakes on Sunday morning. There were two bean pots, one with unsweetened beans for Uncle Walter, the other rich with molasses and crusty with salt pork for the rest of us. At Grandfather's we might have pork chops, creamy potatoes, and warm slices of apple pie. Or fresh-caught fish, fried golden brown. Nobody knew then that breakfast should supply the most nourishment of the day, and calories hadn't been invented. People just liked something to eat in the morning! Such as hot cornbread or baking-powder biscuits with clover honey. Grandmother would have been horrified at today's menus, for she said she liked to set a good table. There might be ten or more at the huge round table, but there was always more than enough. If a neighbor dropped in to see Grandfather, a chair was pulled up and he helped himself to apple fritters, peppery country sausage cakes, light rolls, and, of course, pie. The coffeepot was never empty. The coffee must have been terrible, for the big enamel pot stayed on the back of the range all day, but I had mine with half milk and thought it was special.

In midwinter, Faith Baldwin comes for a visit. We may not have seen each other since fall, but Faith blows in like a leaf (all eighty-five pounds of her), picking up the conversation where we left off when we said good-by. We talk right on through the day and far into the night, and I am glad no tape recorder is around because we skip from the world situation to the latest Bruce Catton book, from the new styles in clothes (we never like them) to what the children (her three and my one) have been doing.

Faith is a companion for good times but also for difficult ones, for her spirit is as valiant as her tongue is witty. The time the furnace went off in the night and it was 10 degrees below zero, Jill and I were in a dither; but Faith appeared for breakfast in her fur coat and said probably someone would fix it in time. When the stove went off, she said sandwiches were fine and cold coffee was good for you. And when we have a flat tire, she comments on what a lovely day it is. Nothing disturbs her inner tranquility, and yet she is not what most people think of as a tranquil person: she is volatile and quick, with moods as variable as quick-silver itself.

She is equally at home at an elegant party or sitting in the kitchen eating milk toast. She loves mashed potatoes and gravy, fried tomatoes, salt pork in creamed sauce, and most of the less gourmet foods just as well as lobster soufflé or trout amandine.

When we discuss ourselves, as we do now and then, she says I am too outgoing; I just love everybody, but when I dislike someone it is lethal. I tell her she has a gift for analyzing everyone she sees, but she can be too critical. At that point we generally go back to our jigsaw puzzle and work in silence.

Friendship is a treasure that cannot be overrated. Some-times as we dash through life, I think, we fail to consider that without the holding of friends (that is the only word for it) we should be in quicksand much of the time. The few people I know who take no pains to be friends are a stern and rock-bound sort and, I notice, seldom laugh. When I happen to see them, I feel a bridge of distance like the Golden Gate is between my shore and theirs.

With a friendship such as I have with Faith, there is a sharing of the essential self which makes one a better person, I think. We are closely attuned; often I say the first word of a sentence and she completes it, or if we are out with a number of people someone will make a remark and by a flick of an eyelash we tell each other just what we think of *that* idea.

Yet some people are surprised at this since we are so different, as people keep pointing out, and have been for thirty years. They tell me I am a housewife at heart, a cook, a dog addict, a cat lover, a pushover for babies; whereas she doesn't know how to measure a cup of anything, is never involved with a vacuum cleaner, has no dog or cat, and never acts like an idiot at seeing a baby go by in a carriage. But I think a lifelong friendship is founded, not on two people being alike but in a deeper sense of community of spirit. Faith's compassion and inherent sensibility and devotion to large issues and generosity are basic, so why should I care whether she knows how to make a cheese soufflé or cope with burned-out light bulbs?

That old tired saying, "No man is an island," is profoundly true. A sea of differences may stretch between two people, but it is possible to cross it if both are willing.

There is a new ski slope in Woodbury, the next town over. It is a town, for it has sidewalks, street lights, the

Louise Shop, a food center, an inn, and the best dentist in a hundred or more miles. A ski slope is the peak of sophistication nowadays. It isn't one of those large, imposing affairs such as Stowe, Vermont, but it is a good short slope with a tow. Professional skiers can go on to Vermont and New Hampshire, but ordinary folk get a lot of joy out of slanting down that slope, and the children can take lessons. Jamie has a passion for it and young as he is, he can manage his small skis very well. I think six is a good age to begin, and I often wish skiing had been popular in Wisconsin while I was growing up. I had to be satisfied with tennis, basketball, swimming and canoeing, and roller skating. We did go to Lake Winnebago sometimes for a skating picnic in winter, but there was always so much snow on the ice that most of the time we spent shoveling. A few folk had iceboats, but I never was in one.

I believe everyone should be fairly good at some outdoor sport—good enough to do it well without being too dedicated. I am glad Curt plays tennis and goes skin-diving at every opportunity. Connie is completely unathletic but makes a good audience. From the way small Anne charges around, I wonder whether she may inherit my love of action, especially since she makes a game of everything she does. Muffin sings and floats about but without the special bounce which goes with sports. My young friend Tommy is handy with a shovel, can do fine carpentry work, and runs a tractor very well, but I am trying to talk his father into letting the boy take skiing lessons. It would be a fine thing for Tommy, I say. I can't argue about coordination or agility or balance—I just feel a sport per se is a good acquirement for a boy or a girl.

A Book of Country Things, which I received from Pat Patterson, is a delightful book for anyone interested in old houses, history, pioneer living, and nature. It was in this book I found out, after all these years, that the brick under the Dutch oven in the great fireplace which pulls out into a narrow passageway was so the homemaker could shovel the ashes from the oven into the opening. They fell down to the cellar, where another opening made it possible to take them out to use for soapmaking. Many theories had been suggested during the years, the best one being that when Indians came valuables were popped in the hole. But the Indians around Stillmeadow were all friendly Indians, so this seemed dubious. And I imagine valuables were few in those early days.

Everyone made his own soap in our forefathers' time. It involved boiling up bones and fat, skimming the grease, and adding lye water made by pouring water over wood ashes. I must say we do take things for granted now. We reach for a bar of lavender-scented oval soap without a thought.

We have, indeed, lost a great many skills during the progress of civilizing our country. I know quite a few men who cannot hit a nail squarely on the head or strip a board or put in a windowpane. And I do not know a single woman who can card flax, spin thread, and weave it into cloth. Housekeeping today is pretty simple, when you stop to consider it. We do not get up in the morning and build a fire in the stove, using a flint. We do not heat all our water in big kettles. We turn the tap and out it gushes. Except for some true farm people, we buy our milk instead of milking cows once a day. I can remember on my grandfather's dairy farm how the big pans of milk were set in the springhouse and the cream spooned off—oh, that cream!

I can remember Mama ironing with sadirons, heated on the range. There was a wooden handle she clipped on a hot iron. Then she ran the iron over a lump of beeswax. I don't recall how old I was when she got the electric mangle, but I remember how excited she was. And the advent of a steam iron was a minor miracle.

Mama cooked on a gas stove with an oven up near the ceiling. In our town the gas pressure varied considerably, and Father was always storming up to the company office and threatening to throw the gas stove in the river and get a kerosene stove you could depend on. It was not to be borne, he said, just when you had a steak broiling to have the gas die down so the steak just sat there doing nothing!

Nowadays, everything works by buttons, and household equipment is made in a steel and glass factory and delivered right to the door ready to hook up. Refrigerators make ice for themselves, and we no longer watch for the iceman to come down the road driving his white horses. If we need extra ice, we empty the ice trays and refill them from the tap and have more ice in no time. If we need nails, we don't make them by hand. And when we want to paint a house, we go to a store and have the paint mixed or buy it in cans, all ready to spread. We don't make it ourselves from red ochre and buttermilk. There are a few old houses in my valley that still wear that ancient red paint. It is permanent, as is the ox-blood paint. I tried to do over a chest once that had been painted with ox-blood paint (this was common). The chief result was a bad case of neuritis for me.

Jill wouldn't lend a hand because that was the year the Japanese beetles came to Connecticut, and the only times she came in the house were to grab a sandwich or lie down at night. This was in pre-Rachel Carson days, but Jill did not use a spray; she hand-picked those beetles and dropped them in a coffee can filled with kerosene. She said even the birds wouldn't eat them!

I agree with Rachel Carson, but one summer I weakly gave in and had the worst of the poison ivy sprayed because the minute guests turned up they had poison ivy spreading all over them like a prairie fire. I worried about Muffin and Anne with their delicate fair skin, specially since they are my own kin and I can catch poison ivy just by looking at it. (It may have begun when I sat in a bed of it one dusk while fishing.)

If you are not willing to put up with a few inconveniences, I think you should not have an old house. Better build or buy a new one, or find a middle-aged one. The really old houses are disappearing; they will soon be museum pieces, which is good, for they should be preserved as an antidote, if nothing else, to the modern flatboat affairs.

I am reminded of my Cape Codder friend Clayton, who is a builder by trade but loves old houses and believes in saving and restoring them. Last summer a church built in

1840 was abandoned on the Cape when a small village had so few inhabitants that they went to church in neighboring villages.

"Clayton's bought a church," Millie told me.

"A church!"

"It isn't a big church," she said quickly.

"I must see it," I said. So we left the cleaning undone and rode down—I mean up—to see the church, standing lonely and lovely in the pale light. It is small, rectangular, white, with a low steeple.

When Clayton came to the house, I asked him about it.

"Didn't like to see it just go," he said. "Maybe I'll take it down and bring it back here. Could make a house of it."

"How can you take it down?"

"Just a piece at a time," he said.

He was still in the yard when a stranger drove up, having found out where he was. The man wanted to buy the church. I went inside while they talked, but I could hear bits of the conversation as I heated the coffee.

"Seems as if that's a pretty high price," said the stranger.

"Well, I don't suppose," drawled Clayton, "you've bought many churches."

The man drove away, muttering, I imagine, about Cape Codders.

There's no denying that an old house and its surroundings are a responsibility. You spend most of your time keeping it as it should be—except you concede that a fireproof roof is better than a roof with authentic wooden shingles which would ignite from one chimney spark.

The children don't want me to make any changes in Stillmeadow either. In fact, I got into trouble with Connie when I decided to put an aluminum door on the back by the woodshed. The old batten door was worn out and, since it opens directly on my downstairs shower and lavatory, snow blew in and wind knifed through and often I had to chop the bath mat out with an ax after it froze solid. The door is a narrow one, a very odd size, but the opening could not be enlarged because of the stone terrace outside. (Problems always.) So I ordered an aluminum door built to size with the hope of warming up the back kitchen and making showers in winter less of a challenge.

Connie was horrified. She always begins reproaches with "Oh, Mama!" I pointed out that the door was almost invisible, that it gave on the path to the kennel and it would be nice to have it open without a hammer, that it was cold in that corner, etc. I am not sure she was reconciled, but if that is my sole contribution to modern living, she will have to get used to it. I don't like aluminum doors any better than she does, and regardless of how marvelous it would be to have aluminum combination screen and storm sash (one of the best of the modern inventions), I keep on with the old half-screens and the wooden storm sash which take half a day to put on and take off and, since no two windows are the same size, never quite fit. However, it means the old house is not upset!

I love making discoveries. Sometimes I find something in the heart of a friend that I had not glimpsed before, or find a tenderness or a perception in myself I had not known I had. I don't know how many people explore the depths in loved ones and friends or look for unexpected treasures, but at times it seems that many of us only skim the surface of existence, partly because of daily pressures and partly because we are inhibited by our own natures. But underneath there is a deep, steady river in every one of us, mysterious as the underground river which comes from the St. Lawrence and flows two hundred and fifty feet below the surface of Cape Cod.

The great blessing of a happy marriage, I think, is that a man and woman have time to discover each other and cherish each other more as time goes on. In most of the unhappy marriages I know about, neither of the partners seems to be interested in making discoveries about the other. Therefore they live on the surface, and this can be deadly.

The world itself brings discoveries almost daily. So far, I have not been able to envision galaxies beyond our own, with others beyond them. Space is literally and intellectually beyond me. I watch the midnight sky, with its stars trembling in the cold vastness, and stretch my imagination until I feel dizzy, but I still cannot grasp the meaning of it. While men explore outer space, I continue to find the world of my Connecticut valley more packed with mysteries than I can ever solve. I am content to ponder them through the seasons: when winter walks in silver over the hills, or June's roses spill over every split-rail fence, or fields turn to Midas gold and russet leaves carpet the lawn.

After all, Thoreau's profound philosophy flowered profusely at Walden Pond, which isn't a very large body of water—just one of many ponds in New England. My final decision is that no amount of pondering anywhere would make me a Thoreau, and I had better have a cup of Constant Comment tea and take *Walden* from the shelf.

It is comforting to reflect that I do not need to be able to play an instrument in order to appreciate Verdi's "Requiem." Beethoven's Fifth makes my heart beat like thunder even though I do not understand the mechanics of a symphony. Keats said, "Beauty is truth, truth beauty, That is all ye know on earth, and all ye need to know." There are layers and layers of meaning in these familiar lines, but just the top layer is satisfying. And although I shall never solve any of the mysteries in the world about me, perhaps it is enough to appreciate them. A life devoid of wonder would be rather flat.

On a moonlit night in December, as the earth turns toward another year, I sit quietly and begin to make a new set of resolutions. My first is to be better organized. There is really no reason why Holly's rabies certificate turned up in last year's Christmas cards. And an unpaid bill in a box of carbon paper. I always put things away, but my problem is that I never remember where. My friend Joe Cassidy comes at intervals to straighten out my accounts and as I see him drive up and plow through the snow, I think, "Well, I better start hunting for *something*." He is such a patient man that he never asks why I didn't put November's bank statement in with the rest. Why was it in the basket of mail to go? Often he murmurs gently, "You really should add what you deposit and not subtract it!"

Then I explain that I was subtracting the bills, so I just continued to subtract. Next year, I shall do better. It is my opinion that if you have no head at all for figures, it is better to have someone who does, to keep things on an even keel.

I hear the familiar sounds in the house, the breaking of a burned log in the open fire, the thud of Holly's paws as she comes in from the kitchen, Teddy's long sigh as he settles down for the night. I hear Anne asking for a drink of water and Muffin's elfin, flutelike voice saying something. I hear the footsteps coming down those ladder stairs and know Connie is going for fruit juice or milk or something—my grandchildren hate to sleep.

Then Curt appears for a last quiet chat, tall and handsome and looking boyish in his pajamas. The talk is idle, rewarding. Finally everyone is in bed, and I take my nightly look at the icicles hanging from the old well house, the drifts by the picket gate. The ancient white house with its steep roof and low eaves looks like a ship anchored in a still, white sea.

What the new year may bring, we cannot know, but I pray God's blessing may fall on us as softly as apple blossoms fall in spring. And then I put out the guttering candles on the trestle table and go to bed, feeling that tomorrow will be another adventure in living!